DEDICATION

To The Memory of Nita
Who Shared My Ponderings
For 46 Years

Written by Will Headrick

First printing, 2010, Rocky Heights Print & Binding
www.rockyheightsbinding.com

PORCH PONDERINGS
BY
WILL HEADRICK

FORWARD

Some of my richest and most profound awareness of the world around me came from older people. These were people who had gained knowledge and wisdom through years of experience. They willingly shared their lives with me, when my mind was young and pliable. My paternal and maternal grandparents, older neighbors, and mature church members took me under their wings.

This book is not a book to be read from cover to cover in one sitting. It is to be read and pondered one or two pages at a time. So, read a bit. Lay the book aside. Lean back and roll it around in your mind.

I pray that you will come to realize the importance of porch sitting and porch pondering as a result of reading this book.

I do not claim originality for all of this book. My experience has included much reading and discussion with people of all walks. It is only natural that they and their pondering have rubbed off on me, as I hope mine will become a part of you. Feel free to contact me at my website or at Willjheadrick@joyofwriting.org

PORCHES

The art of porch sitting began to disappear from the American scene, when our nation started its move from an agricultural society to an industrial culture. After World War II people began to make their front porches smaller, and eventually porches became stoops or little pretend porches not big enough for even one person to sit on. In some cases they disappeared altogether. My grandparents had big front porches, where family, friends, and neighbors would assemble to talk, to share tid-bits of news they had heard, and to wait for the evenings to cool enough for people to sleep.

There was a swing on my Dad and Mama K's front porch. I was an introspective child, and sometimes I would just sit on the porch and ponder. I wish children still had time for that kind of thing. Now, they are playing computer games or watching television. Most have never learned how to be alone.

I am doing my part to restore the lost art of porch sitting. I sit on my back porch. My front porch is not big enough on which to cuss a cat, but I sit out back with a cup of coffee or a glass of iced tea and I ponder. I think about the day's events just passed, or I think about the day coming up. I utter a few prayers for needs I have been made aware of. I listen to the singing of birds and the scurrying of squirrels. Sometimes a friend drops by, and we share a bit of conversation and a glass of wine.

I think our world would be a better one, if people still had porch time.

SOAP CHRISTIANS

I read somewhere that there are a growing number of people associated with the Christian Church in Cuba, but some people worry that this new growth consists of soap Christians. The churches pass out soap, medicine, and other things which are not readily available in the marketplace. Some people are concerned that a cheap grace is being offered - - - a gospel of Tylenol and soap.

I find myself wondering if it is any different here in the United States. Are people coming to church because they want to hear the voice of God calling them to greater service? Are they coming because they desire to be salt and light in their neighborhoods? Or, could it be that they are coming for the things offered to them. You know - - - the entertainment such as bands, puppet shows, dance and drama groups, music extravaganzas, the coffee hours, the pot luck dinners, the picnics, the bus trips, the swim parties, the sports teams? Are they coming for the hoop-la we feel we have to create to attract people? Are they coming for the perks and prizes offered in exchange for their attendance? Are we in danger of being soap Christians in America? I wonder.

DOWN TIME

I live not far from one of my city's most traveled thoroughfares, and I never cease to be amazed at all the people trying to get somewhere at the same time. They weave in and out of traffic, taking their lives into their hands. I want to ask them why they didn't start earlier or what they plan to do when they get there. I wonder how much more urgent their business is than mine. Whew! It makes me tired just looking at them.

I am a big advocate of down time, and I think there is pretty good evidence that God sort of built that need into us. I was talking to my church folk the other Sunday about taking time to breathe and contemplate. I talked about a little lady named Rosa Parks. Remember her? Rosa went home to her eternal reward a while back. A name was made for her in history, just because she wanted to rest a spell. She was tired and had sense enough to know it. We don't have to always be in a fight and resist mode. We just need to know when it's time to rest.

When my daughter was five years old, her kindergarten teacher was a young black woman, who had almost perfect control of her classroom. Having been a teacher myself, I was in awe of her. She never raised her voice, and you could see those little children sitting and straining a bit to hear what she was saying to them because she spoke just above a whisper. It was magic to watch. Just sit and be quiet.

When Rosa got to Heaven, I guess someone said, "Come on in Rosa. Sit down. Rest a spell.

TRUTH

. . . lot of talk about truth these days. People who are supposed to be respectable seem to be practicing hard to avoid it. Some of most interesting debates in college and during my youth were surrounding the question: Is truth relative or absolute? I guess I still don't know. It seems to be that it kinda depends on what day it is. Oh, sure, I know all the arguments we used back then. They are the same ones a lot of people still use.

We like our yea to be yea and or nay to be nay. We don't want any hum-hawing around when it comes to telling the truth. We warn our children about what will happen to them if they tell lies. My mother used to tell me horns would grow on my head if I told lies. "Your teeth will fall out," if you tell a lie. There are no in-betweens. You are either telling the truth, or you are lying.

But, what if our culture were like some others and had some different words for the concept we call truth . . . words that allowed for some fudging. The Japanese, for instance, have a word. I can't remember what the word is right now, but it means something like, "no definite commitment about time," so if they show up late it's okay, because they didn't mean literally that they would show up at two o'clock. In Indonesia, I am told there is the word belum. Belum means something like "not quite yet." I like that word because it provides for future developments. In that country it would be considered impolite to say, "No." It would be far more appropriate to say, "belum." (not quite yet) Have you finished your degree? Belum. Are you making plans to attend the reception Sunday? Belum. Robert Fulghum suggests some other questions that might be answered with belum. Is the world coming to an end? Are you happy? Can we do without weapons of war?

It may come as a surprise to a lot of people that we have not cornered the market on truth. Perhaps truth is relative after all. In the debates I always took the side of the argument that said it was absolute, because I believed that. Like so many other things though, the years and the miles change things. We become a little less definite in our responses. I don't know nearly as much as I knew when I was twenty. I like the idea of leaving room for maybe, could be, wait and see. BELUM.

TIS THE SEASON

Thanksgiving 2008 is over and it's almost ready to get ready for Christmas. Of course the preparation is already old to the retailers and a few ambitious neighbors who put up their decorations three weeks ago.

This year, it will be different for a lot of people. Some people, like me, have had deaths in their families since last Christmas. My companion won't be with us this Christmas. Other people have seen health turn to sickness, and Christmas will perhaps be overshadowed by the rituals that sickness calls for. Some families have children serving in the military, and for some of those children this may be their first time away from family at Christmas. Others, knowing that this year as they have watched their stock portfolios dwindle and in some cases, people have been left with little or nothing to help with retirement. Economic issues are not new to me. I remember a year when all I could afford to give my wife for Christmas was a little hand-held mirror. That may have been our best Christmas ever. We didn't always have a lot to give our children for Christmas either, but it was always enough.

In consideration of all that, the real reason we celebrate Christmas has not changed, and in all of the confusion of the days in which we live, maybe, just maybe, folks will be drawn a little closer to bending their knees. And maybe, instead of taking stock of all the losses, instead of comparing this year to last year and the way things were . . . maybe we will be able to say thank you for Jesus Christ, whose birth we celebrate. After all, it will not be the bailouts, the stock market losses, and the loss of health or life that will matter in the end. It will be the salvation that comes through the Savior. Yes, there have been lots of changes since last Christmas, but the real reason we celebrate has not changed.

EASY CHRISTIANITY

We live in a world of instant and easy. Since I have become, in the last couple of years, the “chief cook and bottle washer,” in our home, I am always looking for easy and quick meal makings. I've found there are a lot of those out there, bags of stuff you can just drop in the crock pot and there you have it: quick and easy. The only problem is that some of these instant meals just do not measure up to good old fashioned cooking requiring slicing, dicing, time, etc.

I still like letters; you know the kind you get out of the mailbox in front of your house. I appreciate well-thought-out letters that take time to construct and take to the post office. Being an old English teacher, who has been out of the classroom a long time, I wonder just how much of that is even taught anymore. After all, it is easier and quicker to just hit a key and send off an email.

It seems everybody and his brother has cell phones these days, and most of them are in use in automobiles on any given day at commute time. The art of face to face communication has given way to quick and easy.

I guess it seems natural that quick and easy salvation follow all of the other quick and easy in our world . . . a kind of salvation wrought of cheap grace. The problem I have with attempting to get people into the kingdom by pushing, pulling, or dragging them to the altar (mourner's benches and altars for kneeling and begging God's forgiveness) are now out of style anyway) probably comes from the days of my childhood, when it was the job of the evangelist to see how many people he could run through the altar and add to his count.

I haven't done an official survey, but of those I have personally seen come to a confession of faith by the urging, begging, pushing and pulling of others, a small percentage went on to solid discipleship. The pushers, pullers, and number counters fail to tell potential converts that they are about to enter a life of struggle and a lifetime of learning and growth in the kingdom. This is not easy and in the journey, there is always pain, disappointment, and sorrow. Commitment requires more than saying "yes", but people in today's world are conditioned to quick and easy.

WHAT IF

I always told my children not to play the what if game, that most of those things wouldn't come to pass, but every now and then as I sit in my porch lounger and ponder, I begin to ask myself some “what if” question like:

What if the church was people instead of place, so that faithful seekers meeting in someone's living room would be considered the church just as much as those meeting in a multimillion dollar facility?

What if there were no VIP's in the church and each person was considered as important as anyone else? All responsibility would be rotated: elders, deacons, teachers, so that no one ever felt that a particular job belonged to them?

What if no offering container would be passed under the noses of worshipers (where did that come from anyway?) and offerings would be given in a container placed near the door? There would be no pledge cards (where did that come from anyway?) no every member enlistment. Everything would be based on faith. Who ever heard of such a ridiculous thing? Unheard of!

What if the worshipers themselves were the choir? There would be no performances taking place. No applause to give honor to anyone but God?

What if the church became a place of worship and study, so there would be no need for Sunday School as a separate entity (who started that anyway?)

What if the church was a place of worship and you entered prayerfully, silently in preparation for the worship experience and people talked only to God?

What if fellowship and eating took place in members' homes, work places and not at church?

What if worshipers' attention was centered on God so the dress, color, creed, background, socioeconomic status, and position wouldn't matter because no one would be looking for that?

What if the church names and denominational affiliation were all dropped, and we just came to be known as a meeting of believers?

What if we respected people's right to see things differently and what if we loved people, not because they are like us, but because all God's creation is valuable and should be loved?

What if believers stopped expecting to come to church to be petted and stroked and what if pastors devoted themselves to prayer and the ministry of the word instead of oiling the squeaks, drinking tea with the little old ladies, and refereeing fights and arguments?

What if being a Christian made you a member, so that all followers of Christ were a part of the same force in the same outfit and "joining" became obsolete?

What if attending church was not a Pharisaical activity, where followers were made to feel guilty for not attending every service and people actually attended worship for the needs within themselves and the desire to join with others in praising God?

What if every activity outside of worship was considered "options offered, or for that matter what if we did away with the church's sponsoring such things as sports teams and cutsie groups that craft and gossip?

You see it was the book of Acts in the New Testament that got me daydreaming about the church and what it looked like at one time. I know I am an old man having visions of things that will never be in this life, but I can dream and ask what if?

THEORIES ABOUT LIFE AND OTHER THINGS (MOSTLY UNTESTED AND UNPROVEN)

Unconditional love is almost non-existent among humans. Animals are much better at it.

One true friend is worth more than any amount of money.

Most modern day American churches care more about one's money than one's soul.

Underwear is often an unnecessary item of clothing held over from the Victorian era.

Seat belts are a form of governmental control.

Go to the doctor immediately upon getting sick or stay at home with rest and lots of liquids. In both cases you will probably get better in seven to ten days.

The biggest rip-offs of our time are corporate medical facilities and insurance corporations.

There is not and never has been a shortage of fuel.

Marital problems and world peace can be worked out if all concerned parties desire to work them out.

No matter how much fame you have today, you will be obscure in most people's minds tomorrow.

People who are impressed with money are shallow.

People on their death bed never express regret over not spending more time at the office.

Being is always more important than doing.

Porch sitting could prevent a lot of mental illness.

The justice system in our country is out of control.

There is something therapeutic about planting seeds and playing in the dirt.

Lengthening your life a year or two by abandoning chocolate cream pie is not really worth it.

Solitude restores the soul like food and water restores the body.

Fat is in the genes. It's possible to be skinny no matter how many fat cells and propensity to fat you have, but you will have to accept perpetual hunger as a way of life.

Comfort is far more important than fashion.

Most of the things we worry about never happen and it wouldn't matter much if they did.

Being kind is more attractive than being beautiful or handsome.

It costs nothing to be nice.

Even if you aren't pretty, you can smell pretty.

When the going gets tough, most people run.

Statements and rhetorical questions do not require an answer.

When someone asks to talk to you, you don't necessarily have to talk back.

Just because someone hits the ball into your court, you don't have to hit it back.

No one makes you angry. Being angry is a choice.

Being happy has to do with circumstances. Being joyful has nothing to do with circumstances.

Silence is golden. Try a day of silent contemplation.

Arrogance is not Godly.

Most people will be nice to you if you are nice to them, but not all. If they are not, move on. Life is too short.

People should be at least as nice to people who live under their roofs as they are to total strangers.

Forgiveness doesn't happen automatically.

Work, play, and quietly doing nothing are all necessary ingredients in a healthy life.

MAMA'S WISDOM

My maternal grandmother had a good bit to do with my raising, by virtue of the time I spent with her. Mama K was not a showy person, but she had some pretty strong ideas about life. She freely shared these with her grandchildren. I was the eldest of many grand-kids and had the benefit of several years of one- on-one learning, even when I didn't know I was being taught.

I often sat next to the wood cook stove in the kitchen while Mama did her kitchen chores, all the while talking and responding to my many questions. One of the things she said often was something most of us have heard at one time or another, "What goes around, comes around."

As I grew into adulthood, I began to question the truth of that because I saw so many instances, when what went around stopped somewhere on its circulation and never quite came back around. There were people who seemed to get away with all kinds of things and people who lived like the devil and always seemed to prosper. When I asked Mama about this, she said, "Well, I guess they already have their reward." I didn't know exactly what she meant by that until much later in life. I finally realized that if what people have in this life is their reward and there is nothing for them beyond this, that's pretty sad.

LEFTOVERS

Following a holiday around my house, there are always leftovers. Sometimes I like the leftovers better than I liked them the first time. I thought about the leftovers we give to God and to our friends and family. In the Old Testament, Isaiah 44, the prophet is talking about the futility of idols, but he makes the point that the human mindset is to think of God after every effort has been made to meet personal needs. "He takes a piece of wood, burns half in the fire to cook and warm himself and says aha, I am satisfied. Now I will take the rest of the wood and make me a God so that I can worship."

I am afraid I am guilty of offering God my leftovers. I will use the best parts of my day for my own interests. I will do my own personal reading when I am most alert. When I am worn out, tired, weary, and ready to sleep, I will offer God a little something.

And sometimes I will think of a friend who is sick or who might need a word of encouragement, but I put off doing anything about my urgings. Then, I will hear that the friend has moved, slipped into a coma or died.

What about family? I will get around to them later, someday, when there is more time. They will understand. I don't have to tell them I love them. They know it. Leftovers.

CREATURES OF HABIT

I am a creature of habit. I get my morning coffee ready to start before I retire for bed the night before. In the morning, I get a cup of coffee, get the paper, and read the news in the exact same order every day. My days are ordered by an established routine, and I have to admit that I am at least frustrated if something upsets the routine. I make lists of my activities and chores for the day. That's partly because of my sense of organization and partly because I just don't remember as well as I once did.

In the church we have certain prayers and creeds that we use every week. We go through the motions without asking why. There's nothing wrong with saying the Apostles' Creed or the Lord's Prayer or singing three verses of three mostly familiar hymns every week. I have to wonder who decided that we would do that and why and when that decision was made. If I had paid attention in church history classes, perhaps I would have the answer to that.

Our order doesn't change much whether it be a highly liturgical church or a church with no printed order. It's usually pretty predictable, and have you noticed how upset some people get if it changes. The problem isn't confined to older people either. If I move a piece of furniture in my home, my two and five year old granddaughters want to know why I did that.

I hear myself saying sometimes, "If I am anything, I am flexible." I wonder. One night next week, I am going to deliberately not get my coffee ready before I go to bed. Wow! Talk about breaking out of my comfort zone!

I SCREWED UP

Laying aside personal politics, our President uttered three words a few days ago that blew my mind. It shocked me because I have never in my sixty plus years heard those words from a President, or for that matter, any politician not caught red-handed in some kind of scandal. The three words: I SCREWED UP.

It makes me wonder what the world scene would look like now, if more people were willing to own up to their own mistakes and take the blame for decisions made by the staff. Humility and honesty are hard commodities to come by in our world, and it is refreshing for me personally to feel I am not being lied to and deceived.

If Nixon and Clinton had said, in view of their indiscretions, I screwed up, it might have made a difference in the outcome in both cases. Of course that is only two examples. Every sitting president has had some reason to say those three words.

The human condition was expressed by the Apostle Paul when he said, "I find myself doing things I shouldn't do; I end up not doing the things I should be doing. O, wretched man that I am." At that point he emphasizes what a mess we get ourselves into and how utterly we depend on the grace of God.

I hope our present president, his staff, and advisors, all the way down to the grass roots politicians that have made our communities a den of thieves and deceivers will somehow have the courage to summon up enough humility to say I screwed up, and then set out to work to overcome the mistakes.

LOOK TO THE LORD

A friend recommended a book entitled, Blue Like Jazz. I enjoyed the book because I found myself in the author's journey. He says, "I wish I were the sort of person who likes everybody and everything. I feel so negative sometimes. . ."

If I am honest, I believe I can find the creator in most people, but God may be harder to find in some than others. In spite of that, there are people I steer clear of. There are people I don't like to talk to and there are a few people who make me sick.

Fact is: I am disgusted with this world we live in. It seems to be an evil time - - - not the first or only evil time but one of the evil times. People in authority lie and cheat and steal. Those who should be role models are often involved in illicit sex and deviant behavior. A large percentage of the population can't deal with reality because they are spaced out on drugs and alcohol. Parents' behavior is worse than their children. How can we expect our young people to grow up to be anything but thugs? I hear of nice, honest people losing their homes. I hear of hard working people who can't afford to travel to their jobs. I know people without insurance who don't know where to turn for healthcare. I am just a little sick of earth. I don't blame all this on the politicians. I must take some of the blame myself. Look what a mess we have gotten ourselves into and we may be in too far now.

Then, I read from Micah 7:7, and it speaks to me. "Therefore I look unto the Lord; I will wait for the God of my salvation. My God will hear me." So, when I get to the position I find myself in today, I guess I am in a good position to look to God with trust and a kind of faith which transcends the decay I see around me.

I just finished an eight weeks yoga class and although I can't contort my body into all the positions, the course helped me to stop, release the tension and relax. That, along with looking unto the Lord helps me, when I don't always like everyone and everything, to deal in a reasonably positive way with people and circumstances. Maybe that's about as good as it gets, at least for me.

INTROVERTS

I spent half my life wondering what in the world was wrong with me. I don't have it all figured out yet, but I finally discovered that I am the way I am because I am an introvert, and it's okay. People sometimes feel uncomfortable around folks like me. Introverts often do not quickly and readily enter into group conversation, and this may be interpreted as aloofness, arrogance or stupidity. Often it is just that the person is not yet ready to jump into a topic he or she has not had time to ponder.

The first hours of my day are usually spent in some kind of contemplation, things like watching birds, listening to a quiet radio show, taking time to ponder and read. If I am deprived of that time, I find my energy running low before the day is over.

I attended a meeting of Presbytery recently, and at one point the total group broke up into small groups. Immediately a few people took over my small discussion group. They offered strong opinions, theories, and conclusions while I and a few others listened and for the most part kept our opinions to ourselves. I had to resist forming the opinion that one or two people were just obnoxious. Actually, they were extroverts who were probably accustomed to jumping into anything quickly and usually with strong opinions. If you think about the Apostle, Peter, I think you will have to conclude that he was an extrovert . . . always expressing his opinion before thinking, always impulsive, and living big.

I didn't feel very wanted in that group, but in reality it was probably that people didn't know what to do with the old man who sat quietly without uttering a word. If someone had said, "what do you think?" I probably would have expressed what I had been thinking about while the majority was talking over each other. There is just a contemplative part of me that keeps me from wanting to seem rude by butting in or differing.

In the church there are probably at least a few people like me who, although they may have wonderful ideas and above average talent, will probably never be asked to be a part of the group. The fact is, everyone enjoys being a part of something where they feel appreciated and where their opinions are considered important. I am afraid there are a lot of wonderful human resources that fall through the cracks because they are so quietly on the sidelines and eventually just slip away unnoticed.

LIFE IS SOON OVER

I looked in the mirror this morning and noticed my face is falling. A lot of it has already made it to the chin and neck area. To make matters worse, my furniture disease is getting worse. My chest has fallen into my drawers and seems to be settling around the middle like a big truck tire. All this observation reminded me of one of my late wife's visits to her doctor, who came into the room cheerfully asking how we were. “Well doctor . . . seems to me everything that hasn't quit working has fallen.” Now, I know exactly what she meant.

I can identify more and more with the psalmist who wrote in Psalms 71, “Lord do not reject me now that I am old, now that I am old and my hair is gray, please don't abandon me. You have sent troubles and suffering on me, but you will restore my strength. You will comfort me again, and I will praise you.”

All of this old age thing just seemed to come on me overnight. One day I felt young and able to conquer the world, and then I got up one morning old and the world had conquered me. How did this happen?

I hadn't planned for it to come on me so quickly. As I reminded a friend this weekend, who said in reference to someone living twenty more years, “do you know how short twenty years is? And I snapped my fingers and said, “Just like that.”

I still have some things I want to do, but I am being reminded that I had better get a move on (that’s not as easy as it used to be either) if I want to do those things I have never yet done and want to. I have vowed to begin at least one project right away that I have had in my head for years. Lord, help me to live long enough to complete it.

CENTURY PLANT

"I've got to have one of those." That's what my late wife said to me as we explored the plants of Mobile after moving here a few years ago. What she wanted was a sort of cactus, succulent looking plant that neither of us knew the name of.

Those who knew Nita knew she loved flora and fauna probably more than humans. She was reputed by people far and wide to have a "green thumb," and our house reflected that. She could make almost anything grow just by her gentle touch and constant attention. She was always a bit skeptical of the human form of life and didn't build trust for a while. She could spot a phony a mile away and she didn't much like human beings who didn't reflect character. The plants and animals were different she said. To her, all of them had character.

I sometimes called her the plant thief, because of her efforts to rescue plants. One time, on a walk in my daughter's neighborhood, she spotted a particular kind of ornamental grass that she wanted. It was growing in the yard of an unoccupied house. She said it was being neglected. I became her partner in crime as we sneaked some of it to take home with us. In the yard of a restaurant, there was an obviously neglected plant, a small, unimpressive specimen. She quietly, over my objections, rescued the little malnourished thing and it now grows in my yard.

I haunted the nurseries around our area until I found the plant she had said she had to have. I didn't ask for it by name but by an attempt to describe it. One horticulturist said, "Oh, I know what you mean. You are talking about a century plant. Come with me. She took me out back and showed me a century plant, and sure enough that was it. I took it home, but not before I had heard the legend told me by the plant specialist. It seems this attractive plant grows and grows, sometimes getting very large, for one hundred years, and then it sends up a very tall shoot and a beautiful bloom develops on the end of the shoot. After its dramatic and beautiful production, it gracefully rests and dies. My companion loved the plant and she loved the legend even though we readily affirmed that neither of us would be likely to see it bloom.

I think she liked the idea of a plant living out its life and having its last hoorah in its declining years - - - very much as she did. She grew closest to her creator in her declining years, and she easily witnessed to her faith by her actions and her words. She was not a showy or pretentious person, and she would be the first to tell what a sinner she was, but a sinner saved by the wonderful grace of God. Her last years made up her hoorah.

RESURRECTION IN OUR MINDS

I don't even know how many times I have read the beautiful passage from Revelation about the beauty of that eternal city we look forward to inhabiting some day. I don't know how many times during funerals I have expressed my faith in the words of that scripture. It is that which assures us that our broken down and wounded bodies are renewed every day spiritually as preparation is made for a beautiful eternity. We sing about our faith in those promises. We console ourselves with those words at funerals.

But, when it becomes personal, we are like children who lost a parent - - - a child that only knows "I want my mommy," or "I want my daddy." My granddaughter asked me again today, "Where is my Ga-Ga? I try to tell her that her Ga-Ga is in Heaven, she doesn't understand why her Ga-Ga would go away and not spend time with her the way she always has. Most of us are child-like in our sense of separation, our confusion, so much that it becomes like a child calling out for her grandmother.

I have believed and preached that nothing that happens, not even pain, is without positive results. The unbearable pain, the crying, the confusion is part of the memory of the loss and then the memory of the departed. Memory is a gift from God. You see, even the child who wants his mommy or the child that cries out for her daddy, will someday remember the times when mommy read to her or the times daddy went fishing with him or the times mama soothed me when I was sick, the way she smelled, the soft tone of her voice.

And I remember. I remember the laughter, the mischievous smile, the gentle touch, the affirming words. I remember the jokes told to make others smile. Yes, memory brings them back to life - - a kind of resurrection in our minds.

"He will wipe away every tear from their eyes and death will be no more." Those promises meant to comfort others are now a part of who we are . . . who I am.

Community means we are in this together. It connotes that we support one another, help one another, encourage one another, and extend kindness to one another. It means we talk, not just pleasantries, but we communicate.

I wonder what might happen if each of us came to terms with the fact that we might not be able to change the world, but we might change our little corner of it. So, what if we approached someone who has seemed un-approachable? Or, what if we did something nice for someone expecting nothing in return, you know: pay it forward, random act of kindness? It's for sure we can't do away with all the loneliness in the world, but we can do something. What about the old lady who sits alone every day in her apartment wishing for someone, anyone to talk to. What about the old person, perfectly well mentally, but confined to the bed because of physical infirmity, lying in a nursing home every day, wishing for a visitor. Consider the old grouch who lives in the community who is so ugly toward everyone that everyone leaves him alone. It may have been so long since anyone was nice to him that he has hardened himself against human caring. In spite of that, he needs it.

I think I will go over and do something nice for the neighbors who never make eye contact. They are afraid of something, but maybe they just need someone to extend good old fashioned human neighborliness. Nothing ventured, nothing gained.

Loneliness is a sickness taking over our culture, and if we Christians believe what we say we believe, we must do something about the loneliness in our own surroundings. I can relate to people who close themselves off, because basically, I am the person who "doesn't want to impose." I am the one who doesn't want to "bother" anyone. I am the person who enjoys solitude and down time, but at the same time I cherish those in my life who keep me from being lonely. If you have no loneliness in your life, thank God for those people who help make it so. If you are lonely, take the gamble of reaching out to someone.

FEAR OF GETTING CLOSE

I was reading recently about Howard Rutledge, the military pilot whose plane was shot down over North Vietnamese territory in 1966. Since I had been discharged from the Army in 1964, the story was a moving and personal one for me. He lived with rats and filth, and he never saw the light of the sun. He speaks of the devastating loneliness.

Dr David Jeremiah, writing in his book Overcoming Loneliness, "Our world has become filled with lonely people. Though our land is more crowded than ever before, people feel farther away from others."

The corner of my house is exactly seventeen feet from the corner of my neighbors' house to the West, and the house on the East is about the same distance. I speak to one of those neighbors and he speaks to me over the fence or when we see each other coming and going. There has never been any kind of in-depth conversation. The neighbor on the other side never looks at me or provides opportunity for me to speak.

How things have changed! WE don't want people to drop in to visit us anymore. We don't want to be bothered or to have our television programming interrupted. When I grew up in the North Georgia mountains, houses were not so close. One's nearest neighbor might be a mile away, but it was not unusual to have people drop in for a visit and a chat.

It seems to me we are afraid of allowing ourselves to get too close, and our defense is to be distant and aloof.

COAL BY THE SACK

I guess a part of who we are depends on our perspective and most things are relative. I had no idea what it meant to be poor in Appalachia until I was old enough to begin to notice that some of the neighbors had coal piles to heat part of their houses while much of the time my dad bought our coal by the sack. Some folks in our neighborhood had adequate income to stockpile their coal for the winter. Imagine a pile of coal being a status symbol. Like I said, it's all relative. My dad usually picked up a sack or two of coal at the local fruit stand on his way home. The fact was, all of us were poor, but some were poorer than others, and we all lived similar lifestyles. We didn't sweat the fact that out there somewhere in the wider world, people had no idea what it meant to buy coal by the sack to stay warm.

For years I would smile, tongue in cheek, when hearing from my parishioners that they had to budget closely, because they were on "fixed income." My amusement came from the fact that some of those people had stockpiled quite a lot of money through the years. Sometimes it came from people who actually lived on Social Security. Now, I am living out what I smiled good naturedly about. The "chickens really do come home to roost," don't they?

But, you know, I don't spend time worrying about the stock market falling and I don't worry about my investments. I don't have any. I don't think about acquiring more than I already have. Truth is, I probably have more than I need even though I live on "fixed income." If I ever reach the edge of worry, it is not about the things I have; it is about the people I love.

Richard Paul Evans, the author, is coming to my area this month. He has written a new book, The Gift, about a little boy, who can heal others but is helpless against the leukemia ravaging his own body. He makes the point that healing is temporary for all of us, because we are all going to die and the investments, the property, the acquired "things" really won't make one bit of difference. The only healing of any consequence is the healing of the soul.

Some of the fondest memories I have are from the days of feeling warm from the coal heater fueled by the coal from the sack, gathered with my parents celebrating the birth of our Lord. We had a little fruit from the fruit stand where the coal was purchased.

ADVENT

I am more fortunate than a lot of people. I have two ministers, both fine gentlemen who "hold my arms up" when I am tired and offer me spiritual nourishment, even without knowing it sometimes. Pastor David is the pastor of the church with which my family is affiliated and Pastor Samford is the executive Presbyter of the Presbytery in which I serve. I count both of these men among my blessings.

Just the other day, Samford shared with me a miracle which he witnessed recently. It was the story of two men, one of them Jewish and one a bigot. They had hatred between them for many years. Through the working of the Holy Spirit, these two estranged individuals were brought together and experienced that kind of tearful, heart wrenching reunion filled with forgiveness and love that we don't see enough of. That kind is a miracle.

David, in the monthly newsletter, reminded me that God is no stranger to weakness, helplessness, and vulnerability. He affirms that we make the mistake of thinking Christmas is only for children or families, or happy, successful people. The meaning and dignity and purpose in life that one would have apart from the grace of God belong to everyone," he says. God's love is often expressed through weakness, and it is sometimes expressed more profoundly to the aged than the young.

I am part of a religious tradition which celebrates the Holy season of Advent, which includes the four weeks prior to Christmas in which Christians make preparation to celebrate the coming of Jesus Christ. As we begin the celebration of Advent this Sunday, it seems new to me all over again. Each year my perspective changes and Advent speaks more clearly to me about the ways Jesus comes to us. This year, my

Advent prayer is: "God, for the remaining years I have left on Earth, help me to be a blessing to all with whom I come in contact.

Advent was experienced by the two men who allowed their hostility to melt away in their tears. Advent is real in times of sickness and growing old and in death.

Like the woman whom Christ met at the well. She came with a heavy burden of guilt on her shoulders. She left with springs of living water in her heart. She came thirsty, and Advent happened.

It seems that all we need do is to come thirsty to Advent, because God wants to do something miraculous in our lives and God will do something mighty in us. We don't need to approach it intellectually. We don't need to bring our riches or our good deeds. We don't need to bring our achievements, our positions or our family history. We need only come thirsty.

OLD HAS ITS ADVANTAGES

I went out to do yard work the other day. It was a job that should have taken two hours at most. It ended up taking most of the day. I really feel that I can do most of what I did forty years ago. My body just hasn't bought into it yet.

My granddaughter told me a couple of weeks ago, "Poppie, you are old." That resulted from her asking me to do something I just couldn't pull off, so I told her I was old. She hasn't let me forget it. I refuse to think of myself as OLD. I certainly don't maintain the level of energy that would allow me to do all the things I want to do, but I am grateful for the people who recognize that I still have something to offer even if it is offered slowly.

I have discovered some advantages in being older though:

People sometimes defer to me because they see me as wiser.

I feel that I have finally gotten it together, even if sometimes I don't know what to do with it.

Life experience is more valuable than any other kind of education.

At some point, a person no longer has to keep up with anyone or prove anything.

And, I have learned a few things:

The quality of life is far more important than its length.

Hatred, resentment, and hostility are non-productive and a

waste of precious time.

Negative people drain energy.

Humor is necessary to survival.

Every day presents new opportunities.

Material things aren't very important and are only on loan.

Life changes.

Cosmetic improvement doesn't change what is inside.

ADMIRERS OF JESUS

A lot of people could probably be considered admirers of Jesus Christ. They probably like his philosophy, his simple lifestyle, his love for children and his defense of the underdog. I wonder, though, how many of those admirers are disciples.

I read a story about Clarence Jordan, the writer of the Cotton Patch version of scripture and other books. He was also founder of Koinonia Farm, an interracial community near Americus, Georgia. Jordan was excommunicated from the Baptist church for encouraging whites and blacks to worship together. When he got in trouble with the establishment, he asked his brother, an attorney, to serve as legal counsel for the community. Robert, the brother, refused on the basis that he would stand to lose everything - - - political aspirations, job, house, everything. Clarence reminded him that the preacher had asked them both the same questions when they came forward to accept Christ. He reminded him that they had both said yes to those questions. Robert said that he continued to follow Christ, but he was not going to the cross. He said he didn't want to be crucified. Clarence said this to his brother. "Then I don't think you are a disciple. You are just an admirer of Jesus. You need to go back to the church you belong to and tell them you are just an admirer, not a disciple." (from Dissident Discipleship: A Spirituality of Self Surrender, Love of God and Love of Neighbor)

Being a disciple requires much more than having a church to "belong to," attending church once or twice a week, sitting in a Sunday School class, and giving a few dollars in the offering plate.

I wonder if the church isn't full of people who are just admirers of Jesus.

CALM IN THE STORM

Philosopher Verlaine asked the question, "Why are we born just to suffer and die?" . . . seems to me if we see life as being born suffering, and dying, it makes for a pretty drab existence. What's the point?

It's true that sometimes life doesn't make much sense. There is so much suffering, so much craziness. I read of people torturing children and animals or killing, stealing, and trying to force their misguided principles and values on other people. Then, there is sickness, pain, day-to-day economic struggles, and the hurt of broken relationships. Life is hard and there are times when life doesn't make a lot of sense.

If as a Christian, though, we believe what we say we believe, that we would attempt to impose meaning on life - - - to take what we have been given and make some kind of sense of it. I know I am doing that when I talk to, teach, or just hold my grandchildren and share my life with them. I know it is being done when a neighbor takes the time for an un-rushed conversation. I know it happens when groups of people come together to share and reason things out. It is happening when people gently comfort one another in the threat of life's storms.

It is happening when people are unaware of skin color, socioeconomic status, political preference, or religious affiliation. So, you see, we are the ones who impose meaning on an existence, which might otherwise be drab and meaningless.

It is true that we are born and we suffer and we die, but the important question is what do we do with the gift of life between birth and death. Life, even with all its flaws, is beautiful and exciting. As I wait with my family for the arrival of Hurricane Dennis on the beautiful Gulf Coast, I am aware of the many storms of life, but I know also that storms pass and calm is restored. I am aware that even in the center of the storm, there is calm and peace.

THE ELEVENTH COMMANDMENT

A few years ago, a parishioner gave me a little whiny doll with the following inscription on it: "The Eleventh Commandment: Thou Shalt Not Whine"

. . . seems to me there are whiners in every group whether it be a community, a church, a club, a political group or whatever. The Israelites were no exception. They had some whiners among them . . . wish we didn't have to be where we are . . . wish we had better and more food to eat . . . wish we had some new clothes . . . wish we had the comfort of where we used to be, and on and on they whined.

Whining will do one of two things. It will drive people away from the whiners or it will draw other whiners or convert those on the perimeter to being whiners. It's kinda like a mob mentality. Misery begets misery.

Even among Jesus' disciples there were whiners . . . who gets to be in a more important place in the kingdom? Who gets this distinction or that favor? And so on we go. In the story of the prodigal son, there is the story of the wayward son and there is the story of the whining son.

I figure it boils down to a decision. We can decide to live life, enjoy it, treat it as a gift or we can whine. I lost my mother and my wife in less than a year. Last year was filled with whine producers for me. My temptation was to let the misery flow and share my whining with everyone I met. That would have resulted in driving people away. It hasn't been easy, but I refuse to let my pity party continue long enough to make me a chronic whiner. Listen, son, you don't have anything to whine about. You have been blessed beyond measure. You can continue to pout or you can come join the celebration.

The way I see it we can each decide to go through this life as whiners or winners. I have decided to live, to win, to join the celebration.

REAL HEALING

A colleague in ministry stepped into eternity last Saturday. It seems every time I hear of the death of someone I know, it touches a place in me that wasn't touched before the loss of my wife. I think about it more. I spend more time feeling for and praying on behalf of the surviving family. I guess it's because I know a little more now about the pain.

When we got a diagnosis of my wife's disease, as believers we began asking God for a big miracle. We never got exactly what we asked for, but we got a series of more subtle and less sensational miracles. They were miracles that changed our lives.

I remember a church member saying to someone in her Sunday School class, "If we have enough faith God will heal us." What a cruel thing to say to someone who is suffering from a chronic illness. This teacher was one of those people, you know the type I am talking about, that jump on every theological bandwagon that comes along and never quite develops a faith of their own.

There are some things that all of the faith in the world will not change. There are many things that, if prayer and fasting would change them, they would be changed. As my dear companion said so many times, "I have prayed enough prayers to keep a mill wheel turning for ten years." . . . and when folks would express what she sometimes interpreted as pity toward her, she would say, "you know, everybody has to die of something." a lady in the congregation I serve now said, "Miss Juanita taught us much about how to be sick."My prayer is that I might teach them how to grieve and survive. Following her death six months ago, her physician wrote these words to me in a note: "I celebrate Mrs. Headrick's entrance into Heaven - - - into the presence of God ---whole, complete. It was my blessing to care for her and to learn from both of you." He probably doesn't know how much those words meant to me.

Maybe, just maybe, instead of prayers asking God to take away the disease, to take away the handicap, to take away the pain, we need to be asking, "God teach me how to be sick for a while until I am completely healed and in your presence."

MOUNTAIN CLIMBERS OR VALLEY DWELLERS

It seems to me that most people decide pretty early in life whether they are going to be mountain climbers or valley dwellers. I think it is ironic that Pikes Peak in Colorado was named for the man who tried to climb the mountain and was never successful and actually said that no one would ever climb that mountain - - - that it was impossible. A New England man finally climbed the mountain hundreds of times and even did it three times in one day, when he was almost as old as I am. I wish the mountain had been named for him, but real mountain climbers don't climb for the human recognition so perhaps Pike's Peak is a fitting name after all.

I want to be a mountain climber, to do things I have never done before, to reach heights that are beyond my ability. I am not content to just dwell in the valley for very long. The challenges that lie ahead of me each day are what keep me climbing, keep me getting up in the morning and saying "Thank you God for the gift of this day with all its opportunities and challenges." That's what prompted me to climb Mt. LaConte in the Smoky Mountains with an experienced mountain hiker several years ago. I saw my life pass before me several times, but I kept on climbing until I reached the top. That's what put me on the path of earning another college degree at the age of sixty. It's what keeps me interested in learning new things every day. There are just too many mountains to climb for me to sit peacefully in the valley. There's a time for sitting in the peaceful valley, but there is never a time to settle there.

The gospel that Jesus taught is absurd. "If someone hits you on one side of the head, turn the other side to him. If he forces you to go one mile, give him two miles. If he steals your shirt, give him your coat too." How ridiculous that sounds in a world that only seems to understand taking instead of giving. It is impossible! Or is it? If you accept the impossibility of it, then you are a valley dweller, but if, by chance, you take on the challenge, then perhaps you are among the mountain climbers. The next time you try to second guess God, don't forget that His ways are not your ways and His thoughts are not your thoughts. Reach out for the mountain that makes up your hopes and dreams. Keep on keeping on. Place your hand in the Master Climber's hand and be led on.

NURSING HOMES

My father spent eight years in nursing homes. He didn't like it. I didn't like it either, but I was simply doing the best I could at the time. I had little support from anyone except my late wife who helped care for him because she saw that as caring for me.

I learned a lot about nursing homes during those eight years. I learned that there are good homes whose employees see their work as a ministry. I learned that there are bad ones, whose employees are lazy, incompetent, and criminal in their treatment of elderly residents. I learned that the neglected elderly are those who have no one to care enough to check on them regularly and to be their advocates.

I don't want to go to a nursing home, but if I must, I hope my loved ones will find one that doesn't smell too strongly of incontinence and creeping death. I hope, if it comes to that, my mind will have gone and left me with only laughter, love, and good memories.

Modern lifestyles do not often accommodate Grandpa living in. No time. No patience. The old American Indian practice of allowing the patriarch to go deep into the woods and die may be more humane than our modern nursing homes.

TABLE GRACE

"Brother Headrick, would you say grace," my hostess asked.

"I'm pretty much prayed up," I replied.

I didn't mean to be flippant or disrespectful. I had already had my morning prayers, which were pretty inclusive. I thank God daily for taking care of my daily needs.

I'm not adverse to table grace, but when it becomes a repetitive liturgy and nothing more, then I wonder. When my children were young we said, "God is great, etc." and I hope they learned something about God and God's provision for us. One of my granddaughters sings her little prayer of thanks. It's cute, and I like to hear her sing it.

I silently breathe thanks at my meals knowing full well God will not bless the greasy cheeseburger I am about to eat in spite of my doctor's orders. It raises all my indicators of failing body parts.

When people make a big issue of grace in restaurants where they bow solemnly to the strains of a foot stomping country song, I wonder if it is habit, exhibitionism, or genuine thanks to God. I'm prayed up, though.

MINIMAL LIVING

Here I am in the bathroom of my son's apartment, washing my face with a dish cloth. You see, my son is a minimalist, when it comes to what some people think of as necessities. He doesn't use wash clothes, so why have them. He uses soap, water, and I don't know what all else. He has two cooking pots and uses mostly paper plates, bowls, and cups. "Why own a bunch of stuff you don't use," he reasons. A couple of pairs of pants and a few shirts are enough.

On the other hand he is a hoarder of technological equipment - -
old computers and stuff I don't know the name of. He has a collection of guns and hunting paraphernalia and owns several stringed musical instruments.

I guess most of us are minimalists and hoarders. We have no interest in many things and we hold on for dear life to others.

WORRIERS

. . . not much can be done about worriers. My wife was one. I guess people would say I'm not. The Bible tells me worry is somehow tied in with faith or lack of faith. The worriers I know seem to be able to separate their worry from their faith altogether.

I read that I shouldn't think about what I will need for tomorrow, that God is aware of my needs and will meet them. Maybe God is speaking to people who have decided to live and are in the process of doing that. I can't imagine He (yes I wrote He because I think of God that way. If it bothers those who are hung up on inclusive language, excuse me please) refers to people who have decided to sit down and wait for God to do everything.

Call it worry, concern, or problem-solving, sometimes the things that keep me awake at night are what end up helping me come up with solutions. On the other hand, many of the things I worry about never happen.

I can say this to those who worry chronically and to those who worry most of the time about almost everything, it feels really good, when you can give it all to God.

USE WHAT YOU HAVE: DISCARD THE REST

I'm sitting here on a white, sandy beach on the Gulf of Mexico. The water is crystal clear. I don't own anything here. I am a guest. Come to think of it, we all are.

I was stirred last night as I read a book by a well knows pastor. He advocates turning your love and attention to God and away from possessions. He recently sold his large house and moved his family into one half the size. It was all they needed, and it allowed them to do more for the advancement of God's causes.

I live alone. Do I need a three bedroom, two bath home? No. I have a closet full of clothes? Do I need all of the clothes? No. Do I need seventeen boxes of Christmas decorations? No. Do I need three television sets? No.

What will I do about it? Honestly, I probably won't do anything today, and I likely won't touch it tomorrow either. Like most, I cling to the status quo, but all this has got me pondering the abundance most of us have.

RELIGIONS

Young pastor shook me up a bit last Sunday. He talked some about the attributes of various religions, and the attributes were many. Then, he reminded me of scripture which has bothered me ever since I walked into the world - - - a world of good, decent, God loving people of many religions - - - scripture which affirms that there is one way to God and that way is Jesus Christ. I get it, Pastor. I know how personal and unique Christianity is, but you didn't take away all that continues to bother me.

I believe Christianity is still a minority religion. It was the last time I compared the numbers. In other words there are many more people who are religious in ways that may include the concept and philosophy of Jesus but not the name than people who call themselves Christians. What about the strongly convicted, who fear for my eternal soul because I am not what they are? What about the philanthropic and loving deeds done by religious people, who are not what I am?

Pastor didn't answer all my questions, but he stirred more pondering. Better head for the porch.

SEX

Sexual intercourse may be overrated. That's not to say it's not enjoyable and fulfilling. Chocolate and good wine are too.

I've had to give up chocolate because of my sugar levels. I miss it sometimes and have wonderful memories of it, but I don't indulge unless I am overcome by a temporary weakness.

My wife and I were virgins when we married - - - unheard of in today's world I guess - - - but we enjoyed every aspect of our relationship for forty-six years. I don't need to give you too much information here. Suffice it to say our years were enjoyable and fulfilling.

Because of circumstances, I am celibate now. It doesn't bother me. I have my memories. A hug and a kiss on the cheek from a friend every now and then may not be rich, dark chocolate. It's low sugar milk chocolate, but it's enough. And it keeps me healthy.

SLOP JARS

Part of my life included slop-jars or chamber pots, as the more elite called them. It's a part I'd just as soon forget except for the fact that these remembrances make me deeply grateful for indoor plumbing, running water, and toilets that flush.

Using a pot was not so bad. It was taking the pot out of the house and disposing of the contents that bothered me. If the wind was blowing from the wrong direction or your hands were cold and you dropped it, you were in trouble. A great deal depended on how many people had used it through the night.

I was rudely reminded of slop-jars during college fraternity initiation. One meeting night a slop jar was passed around to the pledges. We each had to drink from it. I later found out that it had been purchased at the local hardware store and scrubbed clean. It was then filled about two-thirds full of Tang. Baby Ruth candy bars floated around in it. Some gagged and complained. I supped willingly, just grateful I wasn't having to empty the thing.

GIVING UP PLEASURES

It's hard to give up things that once brought pleasure, things like chocolate, sex, and youthful activities.

As I sit here on the beach, I just witnessed an elderly couple, maybe late eighties, waddle and stumble across the sand. She was using him and a cane for support. They unsteadily eased into the ocean waves. I was uneasy. If one went down they would be in trouble, but they giggled like school children as the water lapped around them.

After a few minutes, they were refreshed but obviously tired. When they tried to get out, they almost fell. A beach walker grabbed their hands and supported them out of the water.

I felt sorry for these old beach goers, but I envied the fact that they still had each other to lean on. It's hard to give up that which once brought pleasure.

DATE

I had a date last night. Well, I guess it was a date if seventyish people have dates. A lady, whom I admire and respect and I went to dinner and a play. It was an evening of mixed emotions for me. I enjoyed the company, but I couldn't get out of my head the thought that I was cheating on my late wife. Wonder if that's normal.

Then, as I sat there in the dark theater with laughter and music all around and my friend by my side, I couldn't stop thinking how much my late wife would have enjoyed this. Then, I felt guilty for my thoughts.

Maybe I'm not ready for this. I might not ever be. After all, I got married when I was a mere child and spent my life with one woman.

LORD HAVE MERCY MOMENTS

. . . had a Lord have mercy moment while pondering at the beach today. You know . . . one of those times when you hear or see something and you say, "Lord, have mercy."

This more than ample woman came marching by my lounge chair, and I could have sworn I felt the ground under me shake. I am not making fun. I am more than ample myself. Well, maybe I am making fun a little. Anyway, when she proceeded beyond where I was sitting and I could see the rear of her, I thought, "no one should be subjected to this. What kind of person would impose that scene on others?"

As already established, I'm a bit chunky myself. To be honest, I am fat, but I try to cover up the ugliest parts. I know some people are sort of predisposed to full- figuredness, and some people just like to eat. I can say one thing, if this gal had nothing else, she had guts (no pun intended).

If you can imagine a five gallon bucket of pink jello molded into the shape of a big ball. Now, take the jello and wrap it in a small, tiny really, handkerchief. Put it on short legs the size of porch columns. Do something only slightly smaller for the top. Jiggle it all down the beach. Lord have mercy. People watching can get you in a lot of trouble.

WASTED LIVES

A young man with a promising future was shot and killed here a few weeks ago. He had completed a degree in engineering and was working for a company on the coast. He had bought one of the old homes in the historical district and was fixing it to suit himself.

Four young men broke into his house, robbed him and killed him. Five wasted lives.

I am a reasonably compassionate and tolerant person, but when it comes to something as senseless as this, I just get mad.

My wife had a saying for people like these four thugs. "They aren't worth the powder and lead it would take to blow their brains out."

BROKEN FAMILIES

There are few families these days who have not been touched by divorce, losses by death, lack of communication, and misunderstanding.

I have a wonderful son-in-law, who has gained my respect and love. In the beginning, of course, I didn't think he was worthy of my daughter. Now, I love him like a son. I have a daughter-in-law who, bless her heart, has worked to understand her husband's strange southern family. You see, she is a yankee - - - New York state upbringing. She can't help that, and I don't hold it against her. It takes some doing for a yankee to understand people from Appalachia. She is good to me, and I love her for it. I had to reach the point of saying, “It is what it is.”

Then, there is my ex daughter-in-law. Divorced from my son, but I never received any papers myself, and she is like a daughter to me. My son sometimes struggles with my relationship with his ex and her daughter, but they show their love for me all the time. I'm still Dad and Grandpa to them. That's fine with me. I'll take love from wherever it is offered.

BAYOU BUDDY

She is a World War II veteran, an Army nurse I think. After Hurricane Katrina, she and I worked together in relief efforts in a little fishing village called Bayou La Batre. We called ourselves Bayou buddies. We still are.

My buddy is losing her eyesight, but as with all of the disappointments and setbacks of life, she is taking it in stride. She keeps looking forward.

Bayou buddy recently went on one of the honor flights to Washington, D.C. While there, she was selected to place a wreath on the tomb of the Unknown Soldier. I don't know who made the choice, but there couldn't have been a better one.

I salute my bayou buddy. What a life! What drive! What faith!

You go girl.

THERE'S A SCARCITY IN THE CLERGY

I like good preachin'. That's primarily what I go to church for. The young pastor of my church is good He's working on his doctorate, and he is learning not to be quite so scholarly in the pulpit. I hope he doesn't let the education ruin his gifts. He has a good message, a good delivery, and he is likable. Preachers like that are harder to come by than they used to be, seems like.

I like good preachin'. I'm not much into choruses, ditties, skits, bands, and coffee in the sanctuary. The seminaries are turning out preachers who couldn't preach their way out of a paper bag. They're not worth the salt that goes in their cornbread. Maybe it's cause they are being taught by oratorically-challenged teachers. Some of those teachers used to be good preachers. Wonder what happened.

When all is said and done though I don't think it has nearly as much to do with teaching as it has to do with gifts. You see, preachers can be taught history and theory and polity, a lot of which they will never use in the pastoral ministry, but preaching can't be taught. It is a gift.

GARDEN BREAKS

When I was about twelve, it was my job, when I got home from school, to feed our ten thousand chickens and start supper before my mom came in from work, and my daddy came home from wherever he had been.

When I finished dealing with those nasty chickens, who picked and scratched my legs, arms, and hands, if I failed to get the food in the feeders fast enough, I took a break.

I'd go to the house and get me a large glass of sweet milk, a chunk of leftover cornbread, and a dry dish towel. Then, I'd head for the garden, where I would pull up a big old onion, two or three radishes and maybe a tomato if I could find a juicy, ripe one.

Then, I'd find a shade tree on the edge of the garden, sit down and get comfortable with the tree trunk as my backrest. I'd wipe off my harvest with the dish towel, break a nice long blade from the onion and stick it in my milk for a straw. I'd crunch my bounty alternating with bites of cornbread and sips of milk through the onion straw. I'd sigh, lean back, take some deep breaths. Then, I'd go start supper.

BUTTER

My grandchildren probably don't know where butter comes from. I'm not talking about the artificial stuff we eat that's made from God only knows what. I'm talking 'bout sweet creamy white butter.

My Mama K always seemed to have a crock of curdling milk on the hearth next to the fireplace. When it was ready, she would put the wooden dasher down into it and place the wooden lid over the dasher handle through a hold in the lid. Then, the churning would begin.

Mama K would pull up a wooden straight chair with a cane bottom and start churning. Up and down, up and down - - - chug, chug, chug. When she was tired, she'd let me take over. Miracle of miracles, butter would start forming on the top. Then, she'd strain it and shape the butter into a round butter mold. The residue would become buttermilk for cooking and drinking.

She lived to her late eighties, seldom having had false butter.

"Will, take this jar of buttermilk and this butter to the spring house to cool. I'll make some hot biscuits, and we'll have some butter and blackberry jam for supper."

BEAUTY SHOPS

My mother was the owner and operator of Cameo Beauty Salon located in the hill country of northern Georgia, where she was born and lived most of her life. In her shop there hung a sign which said, "I'm a beautician - - - not a magician." I don't know so much about that. I'd sit on the porch and watch those women from the holiness church go in with their long haystack hair all bushed out and needing attention. A couple of hours and a lot of shampoo and conditioner later, they would emerge perfectly coiffed. A foot high bee hive hairdo or a pyramid shaped stack of perfectly formed curls made for a minor miracle, if I have ever seen one.

Lots of women came to my mothers' shop for attention to their hair. More came for attention. Period. Some came for a good listener and a wise counselor. Some came because they were lonely.

Beauty shops are fine American institutions that save a lot of women's lives.

CONCOCTIONS AND ELIXIRS

When my faithful companion was suffering from severe, painful lesions on her hands and feet, somebody told us about a salve made by somebody in the hills of Alabama. Lord only knows what all was in it, but it smelled worse than three day old dirty underwear.

We started a daily regimen using the stuff - - - applied it to the foot and bandaged it. It took a while, but to the amazement of her doctors, the foot healed. We mixed the orangy salve with prayers. Who knows which did what.

A medical doctor told me about an over-the-counter powder I could get for my back pain, stiff joints and arthritis. He said it tasted like chicken feathers. He was right. I put a scoop in my coffee every morning. I'm able to do things I couldn't do when I started using it. I have less pain. Maybe it's in my head. Maybe not. Whatever. It works for me.

SEAGULLS

Seagulls are hateful, greedy birds. I watched them as I did some pondering on the beach this morning. They fought over tidbits of food, and they squawked unkindly at one another. They ravage our local Wal-Mart parking lot daily in an effort to find something, which they always refuse to share. They prance around like they own the beach or the lot.

I don't dislike them except when they make a mess. They are, after all, just doing what birds do. They are not unlike people, and people have the ability to reason. They have the capacity for compassion, love and forgiveness. Unfortunately, they don't always use it.

I guess we are not much different from seagulls on the beach, come to think of it.

SOMETIMES ITS JUST TIME TO GO

I don't often advise separation or divorce, but in at least two or three situations, I have said, “I think it's probably time for you to go.”

A pastor talked to me recently. A lot of people see me as being wiser than I really am, and I try to perpetuate the image. They come to me for advice, and I try to look wise and scholarly. They pour out their hearts, and I just continue to rub my beard and listen. This pastor was, in my most profound scholarly language, in deep doo-doo. I listened, commiserated, and empathized but in the end I said, “I think it may be time for you to go.”

If I have any wisdom regarding pastor-parish relationships, it is this: If they love you, you will never do anything to make them stop loving you. If they don't love you, there's not a damn thing you can do to make them love you.

BLACKBERRY PICKING

Dad K called the cool snap blackberry winter. It came every year while the wild blackberries were covered with their little white blossoms. Later, the blooms would change to bright green berries that would eventually turn a dark purplish color. Mama K and I would scout them out to see where the most berries were.

When they were ready, we would get our buckets, a cap for me and a bonnet for Mama K and head out to the berry patch.

We usually saw at least one snake slithering away through the underbrush, and we saw lots of bees and bugs. We would come back to the farmhouse with two buckets of plump berries and a lot of itching.

My body was always infested with tiny red bugs called chiggers. These little pin head sized varmints loved to get in wet moist places on the human body, so for me they all migrated to my crotch and scrotum. I would wash and wash and finally rub with some stinging stinky stuff Mama K gave me to get rid of them. "Hardly worth it", you say. You haven't eaten my Mama K's blackberry cobbler or jam.

THANK GOD FOR THE MEMORIES

Most of the time I feel that memory is a wonderful gift. There are always things we would just as soon forget, but in the worst of circumstances, there can be found some good memories. As we get older, we find ourselves often forgetting where we put the mail, the toenail clippers, our glasses, our drink, etc., but usually we can remember the smallest detail of something that happened years ago.

Memories from my college days sometimes surprise me with their vividness. I remember little conversations with a girl named Jody. Wonder where Jody is now. I remember how a friend named Gary kept me laughing, when he really didn't mean to say anything funny. And I remember the Navy couple who taught me how to make wonderful swiss steak from venison There were the people I grew up with: Rhea, a cousin with whom I spent some summers. I think Rhea died. Jackie. What good times we once had. Wonder where he is now.

I heard recently about a lady about my age who gets together with school friends every year. They come from all over to enjoy a slumber party - - - a kind of sleepover. They laugh and talk and catch up. What a wonderful way to enforce memories and build new ones.

I guess I say all of that to say this: All of life changes and we move on to new friends, different relationships, and all kinds of new challenges. Each stage of life brings its own people, events, difficulties, and victories. Nothing stays the same, and the people who have the hardest time with that are those who can't accept it. Yes, people move, people change in their interests and perspectives. People die. That's the way it is.

I ran into an old Army buddy three or four years ago. It was wonderful to see him after all this time, but after we exchanged pleasantries and caught up on family, etc. - - - after about an hour, there didn't seem to be much else to say. Our relationship, once so important to us, has settled into an exchange of Christmas cards and short notes. I think we both wanted it to be more, but we were different people living in different times and circumstances.

In His Sermon on the Mount, Jesus said something like: Don't worry about tomorrow. Don't set your heart on the needs that may arise in the future. In every day seek to put all things in perspective - - - put God where God belongs and wherever you are and with whomever you share life, you will be complete. Life doesn't have to be perfect for those in it to be happy. There is evil, disease, difficulties, hurdles in all the stages of life, but we live not "because of," but "in spite of." Thank God for the memories of the past and look to the new ones being built.

WHEN DADDY DIED

I can't remember ever having more mixed emotions than when my father died. There had been some old hurt between us for years, and that hurt had been characterized by silence and inner turmoil on my part - - - his too I guess. I had watched my father slowly destroy himself with neglect, alcohol, and a refusal to accept responsibility for his own actions. I had become his caregiver in those last years, and his anger and frustration was often directed at me. I took it in stride at least on the outside. When it came down to his last few weeks I struggled until I was able to say, "Dad, no matter what has happened in the past, I love you and I regret not having made an effort to spend more good quality time with you through the years.

I look back now and realize what a kind and fun-loving person my father was. I remember the year he worked with me to make my science project something I could be proud of. I remember the rides on his Harley. I remember how he loved cars and how he taught me to drive, way before I should have learned. I remember his pride when he let me drive one of his cars or when I went away to college, and he let me drive the 55 Chevy.

In later years I became far too judgmental and unforgiving of his behavior. As a result of that, I drove a wedge between us even though I saw him almost every day. If I had the opportunity to do it over, I would overlook lots more and treasure the good moments. I would laugh and joke more with him as he remembered the good old days. I wouldn't fuss at him for his smoking and I would tell him how much I love him, because, as someone once said, "Expressed affection is the best of all methods to use when you want to light a glow in someone else's heart and feel it in your own." I would spend more time with him, not just taking care of him, but listening to him, sharing with him, laughing with him.

I think often of my father. He was far from a perfect daddy, probably not even a good one by most people's standards. He was certainly not a conventional one, but he was loved by those who knew him. He was generous to a fault. The term "giving someone the shirt off your back" was literal to him. He once gave his shoes away and came home barefooted. He lived in the moment and celebrated life with gusto. No one was prouder when I became a Christian. No one was prouder when I accepted the call to ministry. Though he may not have told me often, he told everyone else how proud he was of me.

As I have come to know, the best thing we can give our children is love. Time and patience comes from love. Maybe our parents, as they get older, would rather have our time and patience than anything else.

THE THINGS YOU KNOW

The teacher in my latest writing course says, "write about the things you know," so I find myself writing a lot about aging.

I am intrigued by the advertisements of age defying products, the diets that are supposed to hold off the aging process, the surgical techniques, some of which can be done on a lunch hour, which make people young and beautiful. There is running, walking, workouts, gyms, and trainers. . . seems to me there is a fight on in this country to stop or hold off aging. This isn't new though and probably not confined to our country. I read that early settlers came to America in search of fountains of youth.

Guess what, though. People still get old, wrinkled, bent over, and slow. It seems to me it is far more becoming to grow old with some degree of grace than to enter this time of life kicking and screaming. I remember a man in my old neighborhood who walked without fail every day, until he couldn't. One day not long ago, he died. My old neighbors called to tell me.

Cosmetic surgery usually just succeeds in making people's eyes slant and their smile become sort of permanently plastered on. Then, in a little while, it falls like every other body part. It seems everything eventually falls or quits working, if we live long enough.

It's tough physically and it's tough in other ways. Growing old is definitely not for sissies. We have to step aside and enter that phase of life, when not many people know who we are anymore and they don't much care about our opinions. Lots of the younger generation develops condescending attitudes toward us, because, after all, we are just old.

We can fight getting old, doing things that make us look

ridiculous, or we can embrace it, enjoy it, celebrate it and find our niche in this new phase of life.

I choose the later, because I have discovered that if I stay clean, reasonably well groomed to the point of not being offensive to others; if I don't push my body to things it resists; if I eat healthy food most of the time and throw in a piece of cake and ice cream when it's time to celebrate something; if I take a pleasurable trip now and again; if I keep a not-too-stressful project going; if I read books that take me away and challenge me; if I do something for someone else every day and try to bless the lives of others, well it ain't so bad. In fact, laying aside the new pains and the slowing down, I kinda like it. It's not such a bad place to be in.

I BELIEVE

I have been in beautiful San Diego, California on Coronado Island for almost two weeks visiting my son and his family. Amidst enjoying the beauty of this place, I have been keeping up with some of the current events. I probably should have left that off, since, as usual, I am not very encouraged as I consider the situation that my children and grandchildren are stepping further into, while I am beginning to step out of it.

I watched the presidential debate. I didn't hear anything from either candidate that made me want to stand up and cheer. I listen to our elected representatives as they continue to bicker and make a bigger mess than we already have. I hear horror stories about what people do to one another. I feel empathy for those dealing with the pain, loss and grief that come in life.

I wonder why God is silent. I sometimes despair over what I see. I do not understand the suffering and evil. I do not understand why the most vulnerable and weak are the ones to suffer the most. I don't have nearly as many answers as I have questions. I'm sick and tired of hearing the people who think they have the answers. In spite of all that, when all is said and done, I BELIEVE.

STEALING AWAY

I have a need to "steal away" sometimes. I need to get away from the activities of daily life. I realize not everyone is an introvert who gains strength from solitude, but I strongly suspect that there is something to be gained from solitude no matter what your personality type. If Jesus went away into the desert or to a quiet place in the garden, then how much more do I need that I also believe that Jesus might have been an introvert - - - just a suspicion of mine. My clues are in His needing time to renew by Himself, His speaking to the multitudes but finding fulfillment in small groups, and in what I interpret to be a quiet countenance. At any rate, Jesus found it necessary to steal away at times. There is another hint found in His being so often and so grossly misunderstood. I won't argue the point, though.

Last week, I was invited by some good friends to spend time alone in their cabin on the lake. What a wonderful opportunity to read and write and sit and ponder. I realized how much most of us are prone to neglect this one aspect of our living that may well be the most vital to our being the people we were created to be.

The excuse we most often use is that we don't have time. Well, you know what? You and I have the same amount of time in each day up until the day we check out. We don't always have control of our time, but it is pretty certain we have some flexibility in the ordering of our priorities I like the idea of one day vacations - - a time to go to a favorite place of just to be at home puttering around quietly. Then, there are little weekend get-aways and even fifteen minute trips using the resources of our minds.. I have to ask myself sometime: What would be the worst thing that could happen, if I walked away from everything, just for today?

I want to enjoy the gift of life today. I recently said to my writing coach, that I don't have all that much time for the publishing process. She said, "Well let's look at it this way: You'll go out doing what you love" That's really what it's about, isn't it?

COMMON SENSE, FAITH, AND CALMNESS

They are telling us to "batten down the hatches" again. It brings back memories of Katrina three years ago and Ivan not long before that. I should have knows this one wouldn't be good. My daughter said, "I don't even like the name Gustav." Someone in the paper said we ought to name these things southern names like Mary Sue or Jim Bob. Who ever heard of a southern storm named Gustav?

If I am tired of this after living here just a few years, I can only imagine how tired those who have lived here all their lives must feel. You start trying to remember where you stored your plywood for boarding up windows. You go to Wal-Mart only to discover there is no bottled water, milk, bread, or batteries. I guess they will re-stock at some point. I guess I need to make a run to the gas station, since my tank is on a quarter tank. I may be forced to evacuate. The gas has probably gone up twenty cents just on the threat of a storm.

I turned on the television first thing this morning hoping that Gustav had decided to go somewhere else, preferably a non-populated area, which is hard to find along the Gulf, but that was not the case.

I am the type of person who doesn't get too excited about things. I, along with my family sat out Katrina. I sat on my daughter's back porch and watched the wind tear the awning off the back of my house next door. I watched trees and limbs blowing through the air. It was an awesome sight. I guess I always hope I won't have to have a direct confrontation with the storm but then I always hope that about all the storms of life. Inevitably, we are going to have to deal with some of them. Preparedness is certainly important, and part of the fortification we need is trust in the calmer of storms and to know, through faith, that we are in His hands. Common sense, strong faith, and calmness go a long way toward dealing with any storm.

WE'RE IN THIS TOGETHER

The young ones don't come right out and laugh at me, but they kind of smile with their tongues in cheeks, when I say that God never changes and we don't have to develop new ways to make Him hear us. I keep hearing how the old ways are outdated. One young pastor told me that the churches that survive, in a few years will be built with stadium seating in the round. Of course everything will be imaged on giant screens. I guess that's already happening.

Remember the story of old, fat, contented, complacent Eli in I Samuel of the Old Testament and young energetic Samuel. Samuel, who really wasn't even listening for God's word when it came to him. Now, Eli is old, outdated and sluggish, but it is Eli that was needed to tell Samuel that this voice which so intrudes and confuses the young man is the voice of God. You see, Eli has had much experience and possesses much wisdom. He knows the sound of God's voice.

So, Samuel, with his youth and vigor, is needed, but Eli, with his solid maturity and wisdom, is also needed. I'm afraid that not much credit is given any more to the wisdom of experience and learning developed over years of trial and error, agonizing prayer and growing faith. God is not limited to the old and God is not limited to the young. God is not limited to my methods, and God is not limited to your methods.

So, maybe, in this time when the word of God seems just as rare as in the days of Eli and Samuel, we need to celebrate that God still speaks and God speaks to the little and the lowly, the young and the old. God has plans for people of all generations, and He has dreams for His church. In our age, Lord, in our age as in ages past and for ages to come.

BEACH DAYS, SOLITUDE, AND MORE PONDERING

I have spent a lot of time during the last forty years or so in places like hospital waiting rooms, critical care rooms, intensive care units, emergency rooms, funeral homes, and cemeteries. I am sure that my view of life is different in some ways because of this. Robert Fulghum said in one of his books, "I don't waste much time mowing grass or washing cars or raking leaves or making beds or shining shoes or washing dishes." He says he learned that there really isn't much time for all that stuff. He said it probably explains why he doesn't honk his horn at people who sit at a traffic light when the light turns green. We need to be patient with people who haven't thought much about death and dying.

Spending a lot of time with dying people and grieving survivors explains why I have my times to think. I go a step further than porch pondering nowadays and have a beach pondering day. I am so glad I live near the beach now. I am convinced it is one of God's gifts to me in my last years. I believe God does things like that for His kids. My beach days don't count, if anyone goes with me. I like going to the beach with others, but that's really something different from beach pondering days. My beach days are spent alone. I take a beach chair, sometimes a radio, a cooler of refreshment, and a good book. I listen to the hypnotizing sounds of the waves beating on the shore. I talk to God some and listen to God more. I understand why Jesus often went to a quiet place. After all, He had a lot of heavy stuff to deal with. I am certainly no Jesus, but I think I have some of the same needs he had.

No, there isn't much time to do trivial, unimportant things, but there is time to live - - - to really live, to treasure each moment and to see each day as a precious gift until that time, when someone will hopefully be near in the dying and death times. It's about time for another beach day. I feel the need increasing even as I write.

WHO'S WHO

The longer I stick around, the more I realize how little I know and how little I care about what people think of me. I don't say that to say there aren't people whose opinions I value. It's just that perspective changes over the years.

I received an invitation to be included in the next issue of Cambridge Who's Who the other day. I suspect that a lot of people got on their mailing list. Who on earth would nominate me for that? In the invitation, they said my candidacy had been approved because of my being an accomplished individual. Poppycock! Over the years I have been included on lots of Who's Who lists: Who's Who Among Southern Religious Leaders, Who's Who in American Education. The list goes on. At one time I was just insecure enough to want to add these things to my resume.

Of course I won't send anything in, and I certainly won't buy the book. That's just not the kind of book I would take to the reading room with me, if you know what I mean. I really don't give a flip who's who in anything.

I have changed in my views of nearly everything about myself. I suspect most people do, if they live long enough. For one thing I am free to denounce a lot of ego-stroking. I am free to do and not do a number of things. I wear comfortable clothes now, because I choose to. I really don't care about being fashionable. That means I need comfortable shoes that go along with what the podiatrist told me I should wear. I don't do weight reduction diets anymore. I have been on every diet in the world I guess and they all worked, if I stayed on them. I choose not to spend my life like that. I do try to eat like my diabetes doctor tells me to for obvious reasons. I don't make attempts to be attractive to anyone. What you see is what you get. I try to keep my body clean and not smelling offensive, but that's about as far as it goes.

I don't remember things as well as I used to. Every now and again I forget what my next point in a sermon or presentation is. The appearance of wise old age overcomes the blunders most of the time. I cough and sputter more than I used to, and I make other bodily sounds that make me glad I am alone or with people who feel comforted, because they do the same thing.

I don't like conflict and I steer clear of it, if I can. I don't like big gatherings of people, especially people I don't know and am expected to be nice to. I like gatherings of people I love and admire. I get bored with most movies and television in general, but there are a few things in movies and TV that get my attention. I hate exercise and only do it as a social activity or as a survival technique. I eat things I like every now and then, even if I know it is bad for me. I, like Jesus and his friends, enjoy a good glass of wine every now and then. I spend time with people kinda like I imagine Jesus might have hung out with. I go to bed, when I want to even if it is not dark sometimes, and I get up when I want to, for the most part.

I never thought that this old, sometimes grouchy, recluse would be me, but it is and that's okay. I am pretty much a lovable old grouch, who doesn't care much for notoriety of any kind, not even Cambridge Who's Who.

ETHNOCENTRISM

A fancy word, often taught in introductory sociology courses is ethnocentrism. That word means our tendency to organize the entire world around ourselves. The idea that we, somehow, are more important than others or that God is not as concerned with the welfare of other nations as our nation, not as concerned with other races as our race is ethnocentrism.

The book of Jonah, in the Old Testament, is a rather strong attack on that kind of thinking. God gave Jonah an opportunity to do something good, but it was for the wrong people, at least in Jonah's thinking. Jonah was afraid it might work, that the Ninevites might listen, repent and that God would forgive them. You see, with these filthy people, you knew where you stood. If God cleaned them up, then Jonah might have to deal with them. I think this story is actually about me, about us. We have a tendency to unmercifully dissect the world into THEM and US - - - the good guys and the bad guys.

Most people still find it difficult to internalize the word of God. If He is our God, what is He doing working the other side of the street? You mean God could actually care about the Chinese, the North Koreans, the people of Iraq, Iran, and Afghanistan? Do you mean to tell me that God actually cares about the Moslems who live down the street and the black family across the street?

You see, the story of Jonah speaks to me, not just because of the big fish aspect of it but because if God was among the Ninevites and was their God, then He can be my God. When Jesus invited Judas to the table, I know I can get an invitation, too. If God managed to care, even for the Ninevites, to find a place in His merciful heart for them, then I can cling to the expansive mercy of a loving God. There is a wideness in God's mercy. It isn't all about me.

LITTLE BITTY REQUIREMENTS

Second Kings, chapter five in the Old Testament tells about Naaman, a high ranking commander of the Syrian army. Naaman received healing from leprosy by dipping seven times in the Jordan River. He could hardly believe that his healing would be hinged on such a simple thing. Actually, he felt somewhat insulted that he would come such a long distance for a miraculous healing only to be told to dunk himself in the muddy river of Jordan seven times.

It seems to me that it's often the simple little things that God requires of us that are hard for us to do. We'd rather see and be something really big. Just going to church, praying, studying the Word, giving, and living out the basics of the faith every day seems so mundane and unspectacular, even boring.

When your body or your heart is broken; When you need healing in your mind, heart, body or spirit, the healing is sometimes drawn out and messy. It may not be a dip in clean, living, holy water. It may be going again and again to the muddy waters until we can let go and let God.

Letting go means accepting that our circumstances do not always change but our hearts change and become open to God's possibilities within. After the arduous task of obedience we spring up like Naaman did, with newness like that of a child. I keep going to the river.

TIME

I probably don't seem as nice as I once did. It's not that I don't wish to be nice, and it's certainly not that I want to be insensitive. It has to do with time. I don't have as much of it as I once had. To waste the time I have in trivial matters is not what I choose for my short time left on earth. So, when people make mountains out of molehills and spend precious time on things that don't matter in the long run, it bothers me.

I've heard myself saying a lot lately that folks need to get a life. What I mean when I say that is life is too short to waste it in contentiousness, anger, and mean-spiritedness. I know I don't have much time left on this earth. You may not either. I'm going to make every effort to spend mine well.

PEACE

I am sitting on the porch of a log cabin. I am looking out at the softly rippling water of a lake. The various water birds are gliding in and out of the pockets around the trees. Green is everywhere and is reflected in the water. Acorns from an oak tree pepper the metal roof of my temporary home. Peace.

I have no enemies, God pours until my cup will not hold the graceful bounty. I think of all the precious time I have spent on anger, hatred, and hostility. I am ashamed. I am sorry for any negativity I have inflicted on others. Peace.

I bow and ask God to help me take this all back to the places of hurried pace and impulsive fury. I ask God to help me to be a blessing to all with whom I come into contact. Peace.

HOUSE CHURCHES

These days I am a guest speaker in different churches. Some of these good folks are using up all their resources trying to keep the building maintained and the bills paid. Others are torn by arguments and disagreements. Most are so controlled by tradition that they refuse to discuss alternatives.

I read in the New Testament about a time when followers of Christ met in homes for prayer and communion, and it pushes me to ask some questions which are becoming more and more pertinent: when did we begin to think of the church as a place? At what point did we decide we would hire people and pay them to do the work of the church so that we could be free from it? Where, along the way, did we exchange the concept of love, sacrifice and service for sets of rules regarding lifestyles?

Wonder how many people would fit on my back porch?

ILLEGAL IMMIGRANTS

The problem must be much more complicated than my simple mind can grasp. For the life of me I don't understand all the hubbub over those who have come to the United States illegally. There is the Arizona state law, which has created such controversy, and the president, the congress and most other people, continue to argue the pros and cons while those who are in this country illegally protest any attempt at correcting this problem.

What is so hard to understand about the word "illegal?" I was fined for not having my seatbelt fastened. I was breaking the law. If you break the law, you must make restitution, or that's the theory anyway. Why can't we just say, "If you come here illegally, you will be returned to your country"? You may only come here through legal processes." I guess that's too simple.

INTER-RACIAL RELATIONS

I performed an inter-racial marriage last week... nice young folks, intelligent, articulate. There was no reason that I could see not to make this union legal.

Their baby boy, yet to be born into this world, will face some hard times and difficult decisions. Heck, we all do, don't we? His will have to do with deciding which side of his family he wants to emphasize – maybe even if he wants to live as black or white. Ideally, there will be a nice blending – not likely in our time.

Our president is racially mixed. He chose to refer to himself as black, but he could just as easily have chosen to emphasize his mother's whiteness. His is clearly racially mixed as most Americans are. I am predominately German on one side of the family and American Indian on the other. Then there is the Irish strain.

It's so complicated that it's easier for me just to accept all people as God's creation – multi-colored and multi-cultural but God's nevertheless.

PILLS

They added more pills last week to my symphony of physical ailments. I think the count is up to six or seven. Three years ago I didn't take any. Now there's one for blood pressure, one for cholesterol, one for diabetes and on and on we go. If I live ten more years, I'll need an airport cart on wheels to carry them.

I reckon doctors must think giving pills and doing surgery is the answer. I wonder what would happen if I just quit taking the little aggravating, inconvenient things. I might get real sick and be placed in a home. Lord knows I don't want that. I could die and go to Heaven, and that's a nice thought. Since I can't be sure I guess I'll keep swallowing the pills every night and every morning.

God help me to swallow easier and to have a better attitude about it.

A GREAT AMERICAN RIP-OFF

Cable and satellite television… I watch two or three channels, when I watch TV at all. I'm not into reality TV, so that lets me out of much of it. I figure I deal with enough reality in daily life. Give me something to entertain me and take me away from reality for a bit.

You can't call up the provider and say, "I never watch anything but CNN and the food network, so that's all I want." No, sirree, you gotta take a "package," for which you pay a small mint.

I tried to hook up an old-timey antenna. Even that was complicated. I had to buy a "box," and then I got only one channel.

You can't fight it. We are more and more unable to order and control our lives. How I pray for my grandchildren.

COMMUNICATION APPARATI

If evolution were true, it wouldn't be long before people would have a food intake hole but no mouth and voice box.

Everywhere I look people are pecking and punching on little boxes. They rudely ignore you while they carry on anonymous conversations by box. They text and they e-mail. They burst out laughing like a hyena at Lord knows what.

Even the language is changing. There are more and more words I don't know and word usage that makes no sense to me. It's enough to drive an old English teacher and professional orator slap crazy.

Wonder how long I'll be able to hold out before I get me one of them durn boxes.

LIVING ALONE

Living alone causes one to develop habits inappropriate to communal living. I never close the bathroom door anymore, and my house attire ranges from skimpy to non-existent. No one to offend but my canine companion and she is not easily offended.

I talk to myself all the time, and I have taken to coming up with pretty good two-sided conversations. I keep myself clean to the point of being non-offensive I hope, but I am more apt to postpone hygiene measures than I was when I had a wife. My dog, Chloe, loves me no matter how I smell.

I don't adhere to much of a schedule, talking until midnight if there's someone to talk to, or retiring at eight o'clock if I want to. I take daytime naps if I feel like it. I enjoy my own company. Living alone is not so bad.

COUNTRY LIVING

Both my grandparents were farmers. My parents always piddled at gardening, raising pigs and chickens, and generally doing things that country folks do. My wife was from a similar background.

It's true you can take the boy out of the country, educate him, and send him into the world to do impressive deeds, but you can't take the country out of him.

We adapted to city living by never forgetting who we were and always holding onto the skills developed in the country. In the city kitchens of our dwellings, you could always find my wife breaking, and cold pack canning green beans. She would can tomatoes, make jellies, preserves, and butters. She would chop cabbage for sauerkraut, pack it in jars with boiling water and salt and place it in a dark area under the house to "work off." She would pickle corn, cucumbers, beets, peaches, and okra.

She was providing for her family like a busy squirrel putting away nuts for winter, and like the virtuous woman described in Proverbs.

CHURCH

My early memories of church go back to a white steeple edifice on top of a hill. From the top of the tall steps approaching the main entrance, one could clearly view Grassy and Fort Mountains. They were part of the southern Appalachians.

The congregation was small, and it was mostly simple country people. We sang three hymns, had prayers, announcements, and a sermon. There was a lot of love, and if there was anything else, my childish heart didn't let me see it.

My faith was not yet molested by the world, and I believed. It was a simple faith. Only when I saw many years later that church people could be mean and unforgiving, was my faith shaken.

I wish the church could be, once again, a place for the gathering of the people of faith – no politics, no bickering, and no power struggles. Maybe I'm just an old man dreaming dreams.

TOMATO SANDWICHES

In the south we like fresh tomato sandwiches. None of these green house super market tomatoes that taste like slices of red rubber.

I usually have a pretty good crop of tomatoes, which I grow in my raised bed garden. I really like it when I have enough to share with friends and family.

A true southern tomato sandwich is made on fresh, soft, white loaf bread. You spread the bread generously with real mayonnaise. I prefer Kraft or Hellman's. Then you slice fully ripened tomatoes about a quarter of an inch thick and place the slices amply on the bread. You then add a little salt, close the sandwich, and you're ready to eat.

The real test of a successful tomato sandwich is if the juice trickles down your lower jaw and drips off your chin.

If you want some protein, you may put on a slice of cheese, bologna, or two or three strips of crisp bacon, but there's nothing like a real tomato sandwich made from just tomatoes.

EDUCATION

I am a firm believer in education, but I have some real reservations about some of the formal kind. I hope my grandchildren have finished theirs before they read this.

I have four earned degrees behind my name. I worked hard and long to get them, but if I hadn't learned anything except what I got earning those degrees, I'd be in pretty sad shape. I never walked across a stage to receive a degree except a doctorate. I opted out of those events if I could.

At the ceremony for the conferring of my doctorate, I was seated on the stage near an exit. The program planned by a mostly Baptist faculty want on and on. It was hot and stuffy. I flew away during the singing of "I'll Fly Away." I escaped to the parking lot where I smoked a cigarette with a fellow heretic. I also said a prayer of thanks that I was through with all this. I wasn't. I kept going back for more.

SOUTHERN GOSPEL MUSIC

My wife loved almost anything that hinted of Bill and Gloria Gaither. She found an escape from pain and worries when she settled into her prayer corner (her oversized bathroom on her padded bench) and listened and sang along with those old songs of faith.

A few weeks before her death, I surprised her with tickets to a Gaither concert. She was thrilled.

I recently had a five hour drive to make. As I started out the door at home, I grabbed a handful of my late wife's Gaither CD'S. I listened and sang along for the full five hours. The time flew by, and people in cars in lanes next to me must have thought I was a raving maniac and told their children to look the other way. I sang at the top of my lung capacity, and I had no worries and no pain.

Pretty good therapy.

BOOKS

What are they trying to do to me? Barnes and Noble closed my favorite store. They're coming out with these so-called technical marvels that allow you to read a book on a screen. There's talk of the demise of books as we have known them. The publishing industry is in a kind of fearful uproar.

I can't imagine curling up in a comfy chair with an E-Book or going to bed with a reading apparatus.

I love the feel and the smell of a real book. I love going to real bookstores. Virtual stuff scares me. I love touching the pages, turning down the corners, and making notes in the margins.

There's got to be some old die-hards around who love real books as much as I. Maybe we need to form our own groups and buy up all the old books before they burn them to create some kind of energy to run cars.

EXERCISE

Call me lazy and sedentary, or if you want to be nice, call me southern and laid back. At the rare times I've gotten the urge to exercise, through the years I've found a couch or recliner and lay down until the urge passed.

My doctor is telling me I need to walk several times a week. My feet hurt. My knees hurt. I hurt in places I didn't know existed. Besides, it seems strange to me to walk without a destination. I could see walking to the grocery store, the restaurant, or the ice cream shop. Walking in circles displays the intelligence of a hamster on a wire wheel. Add to that walking with hand and ankle weights or doing the power-walking thing where your hands are going up real high with each step, and there is no doubt we are a culture of idiots.

My great grandmother lived to be a hundred and five. She only walked where she needed to go and that was at a reasonable speed so as not to get too flushed. Maybe I got some of those genes.

BLAME

Wonder why it is that we like to find someone to blame for everything that happens?

I visited with a woman last week who had just lost a second son. She was devastated with grief, and she wondered why God was doing this to her. Last year I had a funeral for a young woman who was shot and killed by her husband. She left four young children. I heard people trying to come up with answers as to why God would let that happen.

I don't believe that's the way it works. God isn't gathering beautiful flowers for his bouquet or taking children away because of their innocence and purity.

God created. We have the freedom to make choices. Oftentimes we are destroyed by our choices, or we destroy the innocents around us by our choices. If we choose to live dangerously following our passions, then we gamble. My writing teacher said to me, when I told her I would like to get a particular book published before I die: "Look at it this way, no matter what, you'll go out doing what you love."

HAPPINESS

Happiness, I believe, is relative. I know a man who lives under a bridge. Everything he owns he carries on his back. He manages to stay reasonably clean and non-offensive, and he is pleasant, intelligent, and, I think, happy. I gave him a little money last week because he had gotten a job and needed a little something to tide him over until payday. He will be more respected. I wonder if he will be any happier.

Up in the coal mining mountains of southern Appalachia where I served as a school teacher and pastor for many years, there were shacks with no doors and windows filled with coal mining families. Mangy dogs laid sleepily in the yards. Happy children played while adults sat on porches drinking Mellow-Yellow and moonshine, smoking cigarettes, talking, laughing, blending their lives, living from paycheck to paycheck. Were they happy? Probably happier than the guy in the luxurious chalet down the mountain - a vacation home tiny compared to his condo at the beach and the estate in his home town - trying to keep up with the market, worried about mortgage payments, keeping up with the Joneses. It's all relative.

LEAVING THINGS TO THE KIDS

I used to have a friend - an acquaintance, really. We were too far apart in our philosophies about life to be true friends. She's dead now, and all her stuff had to be carted away. She had told me she wanted to leave her children something. They didn't want her treasures. It was mama's junk to them.

There will be little or nothing for my children to wrangle about, when I'm gone. I have been reasonably comfortable in the various stages of my life, but I've never had nor desired an abundance.

What I would like to leave my children is an awareness that I loved them deeply and unconditionally. I would like for them to know that I treated people fairly and that I was honest in my dealings with others. I would like them to know I had a strong work ethic and that I tried to fulfill my potential - that I had a kind and gentle spirit and loved God. No amount of money or "stuff" beats that.

CHANGES IN PERSPECTIVE

Funny how people's way of looking at things change over time. I was thinking the other day about yards. A Saturday morning ritual at my grandparent's home was to sweep the yard. We would dig or pull up every blade of grass or weeds and sweep the dirt yard clean.

At some point, we became obsessed with growing green, thick grass. For years I consulted horticulturists, purchased a small mint's worth of fertilizer, herbicides, and enhancers. I rode over my grass carefully on a riding mower.

Now, I feel no need to keep up with the neighbors. I have a small yard. The grass is decent. Every spring I say, "God bless you grass. May it rain enough on you so you don't turn brown. Whatever happens, you're on your own. I'll try to give you a trim every now and then but you're going to have to survive on your own. That is just the way it is. Good growing."

There is something pretty freeing about leaving things alone.

MY DADDY WAS A GIFT RE-CLAIMER

I would have said Indian-giver, but my ancestors would be offended. Daddy was always giving me things that eventually he seemed to always take back, when his coffers were low.

Like the horse he traded for and I led home behind a pickup truck, or the JC Higgins 410/22 over-under gun he gave me. He sold it, when I went away to college. Then, there was the 1940 Ford he "gave" me. It was mine for a while. The fifty-two Chevy Coupe lasted through three months of college. Then, I was afoot again. He never took back the red Schwinn bike. I kept it pretty well hidden.

But, you know what? I loved, treasured, and used those things while I had them. It was enough to know Daddy loved me enough to give me things, even for a little while.

MAGIC WORDS

My aunt Minnie accused me of stealing her pack of Camel cigarettes. I was ten or eleven. I didn't feel I had ever given anyone any reason to believe I would take something that didn't belong to me. Even when it was clear that someone else took her smokes, she never said, "I'm sorry."

I was called years ago to serve as pastor of a church in West Tennessee. I only stayed there a few weeks. I was never loved and accepted by the congregation as a whole. I was never allowed to have access to or to drive the church's van. I was never given a financial report. My wife was seriously ill, and not one member showed any compassion. Both my cars broke down, and no one offered to even get them to a mechanic. I was stuck in a tiny dark office with the church secretary. My house was entered and my privacy was invaded by members. I simply left there, reasoning that I didn't have to put up with that kind of treatment. Not one person of that congregation ever bothered to say, "I'm sorry." There is a lot of healing in those words. We need to use them more.

THE TABLE

I was barely out of my teens, when I pastored my first church. It was an old white country church in a grove of oak trees.

We were trying to upgrade and modernize the building a bit. Being paid a salary (twenty-five dollars a week), it was decided I should meet with the painter and help make decisions about the décor. The painter suggested, and I agreed, that a small, handmade table used for communion should be painted to match the walls and the pew ends.

Overnight, I went from being the sharp young preacher to being the idiot that painted Grandpa's table. The little tacky table was a symbol of the traditions and refusal to change that eventually killed the church. It was a holy grail. Lots of churches have them.

TEA CAKES AND TIE KNOTS

On mornings after I'd spent the night at Mama and Dad K's I would ease in beside the wood cookstove and sit in a straight chair taking in the warmth and smells of breakfast.

After consuming bacon, eggs, gravy and cathead biscuits, I would watch Mama K roll out the dough for a fresh batch of tea cakes. I had never had any before and none since that came up to hers in appearance and taste. Maybe my memory tricks me, but, if so, it's a good trick.

When the cookies were in the oven, Mama K would say, "bring your chair over here." Then, she would go get one of my uncle's neckties. As she watched her cooking and talked with me, she slowly and with patience placed the tie around the back of the chair and taught me how to tie a perfect Windsor knot.

I try to give my grandchildren the same kind of security and sense of warmth and safety I felt at that time.

SNIPE HUNTING

My uncle casually said, as we finished up supper one late afternoon, “Soon's it gets dark, I think we ought to go snipe huntin'”

“What's a snipe, uncle,” I asked.

“It's a bird that runs on the ground, kinda- like a kill-dee,” he explained.

So, we got our toe sacks from the corn crib and traipsed off down the hill to a ravine beside the cotton patch. My uncle, my aunt, a cousin, and me.

“Now Will, you get to hold the sack right here. We're going up to the head of the ravine and chase the snipes down this gulley. They will run right into a sack, if you holler, “Here snipey, here snipey, snipey.”

“How long will it take?” I asked.

“It'll take a while,” he said as they left to go find the snipes and chase them toward me.”

I tired of yelling, “Here snipey, snipey, snipey” after about thirty minutes. After about an hour I began calling uncle. He didn't answer. I sat down on the sack and listened. I heard nothing but my breathing and the whisper of wind in the trees. I was a little bit scared, but I wouldn't have admitted it for anything.

Eventually, I made my way back to the house. Everyone was sitting by the fire eating popcorn. They all belly laughed.

“You shit asses,” I said angrily.

Mother threatened to wash my mouth out with soap.

JIGS

My first face-to-face encounter with death took place, when I was eight or nine. I was shuffling down the red dirt country road with my beloved canine companion, Jigs. Suddenly, an old car came over the hill. The teenagers inside the car must have thought how funny it would be to scare us by pretending to try and run us down.

I jumped out of the way, but they hit Jigs, who was trying his best to protect me. He died by the side of the road with me holding his bloody head. I cried and cried. Daddy found me and helped me get Jigs home.

We buried him and had a funeral. My tearful eulogy was simply, "Jigs was a good dog."

I've seen a lot of death and dying since then. It hasn't gotten any easier.

WHATEVER

The connotation of the word "whatever," as we use it today is not such a bad thing. Instead of "I don't care," we use it to say something like, "I'm not in a position to do anything about that."

The concert has been cancelled.
Whatever.
Your hair is falling out.
Whatever.
That book is no longer available.
Whatever.
There's a huge oil spill in the Gulf.
Whatever.
Idiots are running our country.
Whatever.
You know who is coming to the party?
Whatever
You're sick and you have six months.
Whatever.
Your grandchildren just broke my glass door.
Whatever.
I'm not going to make my deadline for this book.
Whatever.

"NO" IS A GOOD WORD

I have come to a new appreciation of the word, "No." it took me a long time to get to this point. I even attended a seminar twenty or so years ago that helped with that word. I think the subject was given as "How to say No, and still like yourself." It didn't give me the appreciation I now have for that little two letter word, but it started me on a twenty year process of search and discovery.

"Will you work with the teens at summer camp?"

"No."

"Why not? You're so good with them."

"Yes, I am, but I no longer find fulfillment in those kinds of projects."

"Will you attend the rally next week and express your opinion?"

"No."

"Why not?"

"I express my opinions by voting. That's enough."

"Will you come to my party next week?"

"No."

"Why not?"

"I choose not to - - - too many people I don't know."

"Go on a cruise, ride a motorcycle, baby sit for a week day and night, teach a high school class, go fishing ?????"

"No, no, and no."

"Why?"

"Been there, done that."

"Don't even ask. The answer is NO."

PREACHING

To be honest, there's not many preacher types I really like - - - too phony and pious to suit me. To be fair though, I have a few clergy friends who accept me as I am without expecting me to discuss only church-related, theological subjects.

I'm a better preacher now than I was when I was forty. I can't believe some of the arrogant and ignorant statements I made back then. I served a church as an interim pastor for three months recently. I preached theologically sound, well communicated sermons. I've reached the point of saying what needs saying rather than what I think people want to hear. I feel sorry for young preachers who need a job and feel superior in their knowledge, when they leave seminary.

Preaching is not an exact, three point science. It is an art at best and a gift at least. It cannot be taught in a homiletics class, and there is never a point where one knows how to do it. I'm approaching seventy, and I still don't know a lot about it. I'm still learning

TIME OUT CORNER

No greater punishment exists for some children than a time out. That was never the case with me. Still isn't. Send me to my corner, and I'll meditate and contemplate until the cows come home. Allow me to have a book, and I'll kiss your feet.

I have a time out corner under an old oak tree in my backyard. It consists of a small metal glider placed on cement pavers with a rusty table to hold my refreshment. I go there, when the world gets heavy. I go there, when a loved one dies. I go there, when I hear of animal abuse. I go there, when I'm weary. I sit and contemplate and process until I'm ready to re-enter the world and be nice.

Everyone needs a time-out corner.

THE DAY SHE DIED

I had become a care-giver for my wife of forty-six years. She had struggled with an auto-immune disease for seventeen of those years. Her body slowly weakened as she fought with everything in her to stay with me. She was always appreciative of the increasing number of care-giving tasks I had to do for her.

We had been to church the Sunday before she died, and we were planning to go on that Sunday morning of her death. She died peacefully. I held her and kissed her as her spirit departed her body. My world crumbled.

We had married when we were teenagers. Ours was a warm, soft, and passionate relationship. My life changed forever. I attempted to push myself through the stages of grief. It didn't work. I backed up and started over. The process continued for two years. I reached acceptance. It was tough. Still is.

BINGO

And the Bingo fiasco continues in the state of Alabama. A Tsar has been appointed by the Governor to exercise a heavy hand to wipe out Bingo parlors.

. . . seems to me we have a lot of really serious problems going on in our state and the world. The war continues to take the lives of young men and women. Unemployment and the economy create insurmountable problems for the most vulnerable in our society.

And our leaders are fighting Bingo. There's something wrong with this picture, but it's pretty normal for Alabama I guess.

CHRISTIAN CRUSADERS

In the last few weeks, I have been available to four individuals who wanted to discuss the state of the church. They were concerned about declining numbers and decreasing resources.

The people who often fall victim to these crusaders are the pastors. It is almost always someone else that should be doing something to save their beloved church, which, by the way, is a circle of like-minded people and a sacred building.

No mention of the kingdom of God and our place in it. No mention of the love of God. No mention of personal failures or mistakes.

These folks are on a crusade to pressure their vision of what the church is, sometimes even at the expense of hurting and destroying real people - - - people who bleed real blood and shed real tears.

EXPENDIBLE COMPONENTS

The modern view seems to be that a church is formed when there are a few (at least) like-minded people, a building, temporary or permanent, and a pastor who preaches well, miraculously knows who want to be visited and visits them whether they have a need or not. He (most don't want a she) dresses well, is active in the community, lives in a nice house, drives a nice car, doesn't offend people, especially the moneyed ones, and the numbers and the giving must increase under his leadership.

It is always understood that he is not really a permanent part of the community, and he is expendable. Like a coach whose team has a losing season, he will have to go. Let him go wounded and whimpering off into the scary world. He is, after all, temporary.

HALLOWED PLACES

The hay loft of my grandparents barn. A dirt road wandering through the woods walked with a friend. A warm bed on a cold night. Feeling the warmth and taking on the pleasant smells of a lover. Sitting on the porch of a log cabin looking over a lake.

These have become hallowed places in my memory. I think it's because of the sense of safety that overcomes, almost overwhelms, even for a moment. Like, feeling the breath of God and knowing everything is going to be okay.

AN ABSOLUTE PASTORAL REQUIREMENT

When I am asked what one quality a pastor must have, I always say," the ability to laugh at self and to not take self too seriously."

My personal blunders in and out of the pulpit have been the food for much giggling and snickering - - - mine and those around me.

"The wheels are fight for harvest," I challenged at the end of a particularly poignant sermon, "but the laborers are phew."

Another time I tried to conjure up the voice of God as God spoke to Moses, "Moses, take off your FEET, for the ground on which you stand is holy ground."

I issued a serious scriptural call to worship, "Come unto me all you who are in labor, and I will give you rest." I was holding out my arms in a dramatic gesture Laughter overtook me, and the congregation burst into spontaneous snorts. Actually, it was a good way to begin worship.

VOICES FROM BEYOND

My late wife spoke to me again last night. At these times she usually just reassures me of her love and support. Sometimes she clues me into things.

I used to be skeptical of people who made those kinds of claims, and I once refused to talk about these experiences. Now, it doesn't matter if people think I'm crazy. There are many who have been sure of my craziness for years.

One time she directed me to a song on a CD. By using the words of the song, she assured me that she had crossed over and was waiting for my arrival. "Live your life and in a little while we will be together again", she said.

I once thought these things were the ramblings of overzealous, religious nuts. I don't know how it happens, and I don't care. I'm just glad it does.

RELATIONSHIP PROBLEMS

A young couple is having marital problems. I could see it before I knew it. They have young children. I wish I knew how to help. Mistakes have been made. I don't know if it's fixable or not.

There have been financial struggles. They've spent less time together. I expect having the children has limited intimacy and quality time together.

I'd like to tell them it's worth saving. I'd like to show them how to work at it. I'd like to encourage them and tell them how important forgiveness is. I'd like to give them the benefit of my forty six years in a reasonably solid marriage.

But, for now I'm just an old man who really can't understand the ups and downs of a modern marriage. For now.

THE CHURCH DOG

Pepper, our overweight mongrel, thought she had as much business in and around the church as anyone else. She often waited patiently outside the rear entrance, while I worked in the church office.

One hot Sunday morning, the door of the church had been left slightly ajar by someone. About half way through the sermon, Pepper walked in, smiled at me, walked slowly to the altar and plopped herself down. People laughed and obviously wondered what I was going to do.

"Good morning, Pepper." I'm glad you came to church today, which is more than I can say for some of our wayward members."

I proceeded with my sermon. Pepper placed her chin on her paws, listening and perhaps praying. In reality she joined some of our members in a nap.

RE-ENTERING THE WORLD

I sit here this August morning on the front porch of the cabin, my coffee mug resting on the rail, my faithful dog at my feet. There is a cacophony of sounds made by tiny creatures with noise makers built in. It is a symphony dotted by crescendos and decrescendos. A white water bird of some sort just dipped heavily into the lake for his breakfast. She has created a perfect pattern of ripples. Cranes with long legs move, as if in slow motion, around the water perimeters seeking treats that are unaware they are about to be eaten. There are no human sounds other than the occasional creaking of my rocking chair.

In a few days I will be forced to re-enter the world. It will need to be a slow re-entry like an ocean diver surfacing after a time in the deep.

I will hold to the peace of this place, and one day my spirit will dwell in a place such as this. Heaven.

PHARISEES AND SADDUCEES

I don't know why I should expect the Pharisees and Sadducees to be any different today than they were in Jesus' time. The church powers that be continue to try and stop the message and destroy the messenger.

I seem to have fallen into a kind of ministry to the down-trodden. I have spoken this week to three hurting ministers. There are numerous others wounded and searching for a safe place to crawl. Why in the world would a group of Christians receive a bearer of good news into their midst, pretend to love the message and the messenger. Then, deceive, inflict pain, beat the hell out of him or her at least figuratively, kick them out and search for someone else to draw in and hurt the first time they are disappointed.

There's a special place in hell for folks who intentionally or unintentionally make this kind of torture their mission.

GOSSIP

I have never been averse to listening to interesting tid-bits of news given by overzealous reporters or friends who know something I don't. Some call it gossip. I prefer to call it unharmful exchange of information. I've noticed that some who claim to never gossip, nevertheless, will sit on the edge of their seat, if someone shares new and interesting information.

Is it true? And will it hurt anyone? Should be the test questions for our exchanges. That being said, we know our information doesn't always meet the criteria.

In the case of the pious, nose in the air, gossip-resistant claiming snobs, I say, "Phooey. You are the worst kind. Closet gossips.

So, bring it on. It will give me more fodder for pondering. Tell me some stuff I don't know.

THE SPRING HOUSE

At the foot of the hill below my grandparents farm house was a small slotted room built over a spring branch. It was shaded by big trees. A stream of ice cold water ran through the room, giving off a breath of cold air to any who entered.

"Will, go to the spring house and bring up a jar of milk and a round of butter for supper," my Mama K would say.

And I would traipse down the hill and bring up the pure white butter molded into a perfect round along with milk pulled from the teats of the old milk cow the evening prior.

There was no refrigerator, no electric or gas range, no dishwasher, no disposal, and yet life seemed to move at a slower pace with more accomplished. Wonder why?

LINDA WAS HER NAME

I was eight years old and in fourth grade. She was nine and a provocative blond even then. We were both what is now called latchkey kids. In other words our parents worked, and we were on our own for a short time after school.

Linda came home with me one day. I envisioned playing together. She had a different kind of playing in mind. When she kissed me on the lips, I became aroused and confused. She said, "You don't even know how to kiss." With that, she went home leaving me deflated.

She went on to make a name for herself in the beauty pageant circuit. The last I heard of her, she was Miss Talledega 500. I lost track of her after that.

Every now and then I wish I had said in response to her discovering I knew nothing about kissing, "Then why don't you teach me," but I missed my opportunity. I wasn't nearly as sophisticated and knowledgeable as she. Wonder where she is now. Wonder if she's still a blond bombshell. Probably not - - - she's pushing seventy.

THREE YEARS IN A MORTUARY

It was to be my "retirement profession." People ask me why I would want to fool with dead people. I tell them I had fooled with live people for forty years, and I was tired of that. So, I became a licensed embalmer of bodies and a director of funerals.

I didn't set out to be licensed, certified, and all that. I just wanted to be one of those somber-looking stiffs dressed in black that open the door for you at the funeral home when you go for the viewing of a friend or relative. But, no, I went all out and became a student again at sixty. It was tough. Human anatomy, chemistry almost killed me, and it didn't help that the department head was an impudent turd who wore his pants too short and wanted to look down his nose at every student in the program. I was probably more educated than he was. I was a little older than he was and a hell of a lot nicer. I had considerable more social skills and I had more experience in more things than he will have time to get before he dies. The first time my wife saw him, she said, "Oh, my, I was expecting a giant. He's just a little man, who looks like he's expecting a flood."

I survived the program and passed the state and national board exams, and spent three years in a mortuary.

Funeral people are all a little crazy, and I say that with affection. Their humor, camaraderie, and willingness to help are what kept me going during that time. My ministerial skills helped, because I often met people when they were hurting, vulnerable, and confused.

I still keep my licenses up to date, but I'll not likely use them again. I'm too close to crossing over myself to dwell on it every day.

LITTLE JOYS

Yesterday a friend called to chat. Before he hung up he said, "I love you." Strange, some might think, coming from one man to another. I knew what he meant, and I replied, "I love you too, my friend." It was an expression of deep appreciation and respect from one human being to another.

I met with old friends last night. We had a few drinks, hugged, remembered, told stories, and laughed. I'll do that again today with different friends. It doesn't get much better.

Now, I'm on the porch again, pondering, remembering, taking it all in and processing it.

It won't be long before one, two and then more of us will begin to make preparations for leaving. My body is already letting me know the areas in which I have abused it. Old friends go on, and I am sad. But, I will also rejoice that my late wife will be laughing with my friends.

Soon, we will all be together again.

WHEN THE TIME COMES

I'm not one of those who want to hold onto life at all costs. Oh, I know life is precious, and I realize it's God-given. We've allowed things to get out of hand though, with all the gadgets, tubes, and injectables meant to stretch life beyond where it's meant to be stretched. Then, it becomes no life at all. We've allowed the Hippocratic Oath to become a document that pushes some doctors to play God.

If I could choose I would die at home in my bed. When I no longer have quality, let me go where the quality is. If my mind goes and I lose control of bodily functions, let me go. Don't take me where they will stick and probe and resuscitate a damaged and failing body. When the time comes, let me go.

THE HOUSE ONCE LIVED IN

I made the incision in the neck area and probed around for the carotid artery, so I could stick an instrument into it for the embalming fluids to flow through. She had been my friend. This was the shell she moved out of earlier today. I had already washed her body and her hair and applied necessary skin lubricants. I had inserted plastic pieces in her mouth and eyes to make her appear "natural," and I had pushed and shaped her face into a pleasant expression. She had been sick a long time, and her body resisted emptying itself of its blood and accepting the preservatives. I labored for hours to reach an acceptable standard.

Later. I would cut down the back of her pretty gown and dress her for her last meeting with friends and family. I would curl her hair and apply make-up to make her pretty.

She was already gone. I remembered her humor. "Will, you'll be the last one to let me down." I smiled as I worked on while listening to Norah Jones on the CD. I sung along. Finally, I stood back and observed my work. Not bad for the empty house my friend had moved out of.

KILLING BABIES

Some say abortion is killing babies. There's the arguments pro and con about when fetuses become babies. There are the marches and protests and attacks and murders surrounding the issue. I've never had the luxury of being able to do much marching except when I was in high school band or in the Army.

I'm not in favor of taking innocent lives. But, I do wonder. I wonder about innocents born into the homes of drug addicted and mentally challenged parents, where they abuse and sometimes torture, neglect, and kill. I wonder about how I'd feel if my daughter or wife were raped by a criminally insane mad man. I wonder how I'd feel, if I had to make a decision between saving my wife or my baby. I wonder if people are compassionate toward the babies or if they just want to expand their political views. I wonder.